TUSCAN HERITAGE

TUSCAN HERITAGE

by

MARJORIE JEBB

With an Introduction by
Vernon Bartlett
and illustrations by
the author

LONDON
VICTOR GOLLANCZ LTD
1976

© Marjorie Scaretti 1976

ISBN 0 575 02160 8

The poem on page 123 is from Arthur Waley's *170 Chinese Poems* (1918) and is reprinted by courtesy of the publisher, Messrs Constable.

Printed in Great Britain by
The Camelot Press Ltd, Southampton

*Dedicated to Barbara Green,
and also to Virginia and Lorenzo,
heirs to much beauty
and many problems*

ILLUSTRATIONS

Plates: pen and wash
Following page 96

A street in Rome
Rome: Piazza Navona
Piazza Navona: detail of the Bernini fountain
Villa Medici from the Pincio at the top of the Spanish Steps
The roofs of Rome—hiding places for many refugees
Piazza Navona from the rooftops
The figures of Castor and Pollux from the Capitol, and the Gesù church in the distance
Rome: roofscape

Drawings

Il Trebbio from 'Corte'	*end paper*
A Medici crest from Il Trebbio	*page* 13
Cosimo de Medici	15
Lorenzo de Medici	18
Michelozzo Michelozzi	21
Vines at Il Trebbio	24
A Medici crest from Il Trebbio	28
Cardinal Carlo de Medici	29
The crest of Piero de Medici	36
The crest of Lorenzo de Medici	42
Rome: Piazza Navona	46
A booth at the Piazza Navona	55
Another Medici crest	57
The Lily of Florence	72
A Tuscan doorway	84
A Tuscan peasant	93
Giovanni delle Bande Nere	113
Maria Salviati	114

All drawings unlisted are of Il Trebbio

INTRODUCTION

MARJORIE JEBB—or Marjorie Scaretti to those of us who have known her in Italy—has written a remarkable book. It is, in the first place, a fascinating autobiography by an Englishwoman, well known in Roman society, where her Italian husband was a banker, and it covers the three most important periods of Italy's history in this century—the mid-years of Fascism, the lean and dangerous years of the war, and the period of the so-called 'Italian miracle', very similar to the English Industrial Revolution in the eighteenth century. The book has humour; it has courage—which was necessary for an Englishwoman with two small children in an 'enemy' country in wartime; and above all it has a reasoned, but not sentimental, love for the Italian people. Of course, other English writers have produced books about their experiences in wartime Italy, but I have read none that revealed a more sympathetic understanding.

But this book is important for a second reason. Shortly before the war the Scarettis bought Il Trebbio, an abandoned castle some eighteen miles north of Florence and about fifteen hundred feet above sea-level. It is so exceptional a castle that its magnificent tower provides the picture on the cover of Sir Harold Acton's *Tuscan Villas*. And it is historically and architecturally important: many of the Medici family spent part of their lives there, and it was Cosimo the Elder's favourite architect, Michelozzo, who transformed it in the fifteenth century from a twelfth-century stronghold into a beautiful castle, whose crenellated tower dominates the valley of the Mugello and the road which was the chief link between Bologna and Florence in the days before carriage roads.

The Scarettis set out to restore this ruined castle, using methods and techniques rather similar to those that Michelozzo must have used four centuries before them. The decaying farms were restored and, with this restoration, came a revival of pride in work on the land which was immensely important during the war. From the castle terrace shaded by centuries-old cypresses it was possible to watch the German army vehicles down in the valley, and if any of them turned up the rough road towards Il Trebbio the cattle were driven farther into the deep forest until danger had passed. During and after the war, the Scarettis made of Il Trebbio a place which the more artistic members of the Medici family would have understood and appreciated.

The migration from the farms to the factories has been much more rapid and drastic in Italy than in most other countries. But in these steep valleys of the Apennines mechanization has not brought to agriculture the advantages that it had brought to the plains, and many farmhouses are crumbling into ruins while their land lies untended. One might expect the changes in the old order to sadden the last pages of this book. But this is not the case. Il Trebbio is one of those rare buildings in which even the occasional visitor has a feeling of continuity, of association with people who lived there long ago. The Medicean period was by far the greatest period of history since the Dark Ages, and today's owners of Il Trebbio have served the place well. This is why I venture to commend this book.

LUCCA, 1975   VERNON BARTLETT

TUSCAN HERITAGE

CHAPTER I

A SMALL WHITE candle was lit and placed on a long table in front of a dais occupied by an elderly man in a black gown, sitting behind a desk. The room was rather bare, and the windows were high on the whitewashed walls. The ceiling was arched with seventeenth-century Florentine vaulting, though the scene being played out against this background was a judiciary sale in Florence in the twentieth century.

The two contestants for the property which was being sold on this day of August 1936 were standing at the table facing the auctioneer, with a few other interested people occupying seats along the walls. All eyes were intent on the candle-flame, since during the nine minutes which it took to burn either of the potential buyers was entitled to raise his bid. One of these men was of middle height, with a remarkable classical profile; the other was a Florentine lawyer acting on behalf of his client. The former had raised his bid, the light burned on for the allotted time, there were some murmurs of dissent, and then silence. The candle flickered and went out—the sale was over.

'For whom do you buy this property?' asked the auctioneer of the buyer, whom he knew to be the Roman banker Enrico Scaretti.

'*Per me stesso*' ('for myself'), came the answer.

The properties which changed hands that day, the *castelli* of Cafaggiolo and Il Trebbio, had once belonged to the Medici, in their heyday and their decline. Situated in the foothills of the Apennines, they look east straight across the fertile upland plain of the Mugello towards the main range of the mountains. Cafaggiolo lies rather low, a vast, somewhat truncated pile which has lost its main tower and moat and most of the encircling walls, while Il Trebbio, as we first saw it, was a romantic near-ruin perched high on a spur of land jutting out from the wooded hills, then sloping down to Cafaggiolo and on towards the village of San Piero a Sieve, the place of origin of the Medici family.

I had not long been married, and, being a country-lover, had suggested a cottage in the country so that we could sometimes escape from Rome, where we normally lived. It was in September that we approached Il Trebbio—which I had not yet seen—on horseback; and, leaving the animals on the little piazza below the *castello*, we walked up the wide, cypress-lined ramp. There—sombre, almost black, and hedged about with impenetrable jungle—rose the square tower of the *castello*. My cottage in the country!

Up the slope and through the high, rusty iron gate came hurrying a dark-haired young woman, the daughter of the old gamekeeper Olinto, holding in her hand a large, antique and very battered key. Through a side door we entered an airy vaulted passage-way opening on to the small derelict courtyard. The paving-stones were broken and scattered, weeds flourished, and the two-arched loggia was being used as a sheep-pen. Our guide had prudently provided herself with a candle, and we walked through our new domain, opening shutters which creaked or fell apart. Some of the windows had been boarded up, and many of the leaded window-panes were missing. Avoiding holes in the floor-boards we inspected the well-proportioned rooms and the excellent architectural lay-out round the central court, and then went up to the rampart-walk, roofed, as was the tower, where bats were disturbed from their slumbers and a hawk flew silently away.

Enrico went down to talk to the old gamekeeper while I marvelled at the breath-taking expanse to the north, the east and the south. But when I looked down on to the old farm-buildings directly below me, built against the *castello* wall amid the tangle of nettles and scrub, it was far less inspiring, and my heart sank. None the less, there was nothing eerie or sinister about the place;

uninhabited for about fifty years, it seemed just to be waiting for someone to restore it to life.

Slowly and carefully retracing my steps I arrived back at the base of the tower, and, noticing a dilapidated doorway in a high wall, peeped through and went down some steps. A surprise awaited the somewhat confused new owner. There, stretching down by the side of the kitchen-garden, was the most beautiful, vine-covered fifteenth-century pergola, with columns made of semi-circular bricks of lovely colours and set on supporting low

Cosimo Pater Patriae

walls. So perfect was it, so redolent of its history, that I seemed to see some of the legendary Medici and their entourage walking up and down, discussing and disputing in the shade of the vines. Later, as I came to know more of the history of the *castello*, this same sense of contact with the past was always with me.

Il Trebbio (the name derives from the Latin *trivium*, or three ways) had been built in 1427 for Cosimo de Medici, known as *Pater Patriae*. It was constructed on the foundations of what had once been a Longobard stronghold, probably belonging to the powerful mediaeval family of the Ubaldini. The square tower,

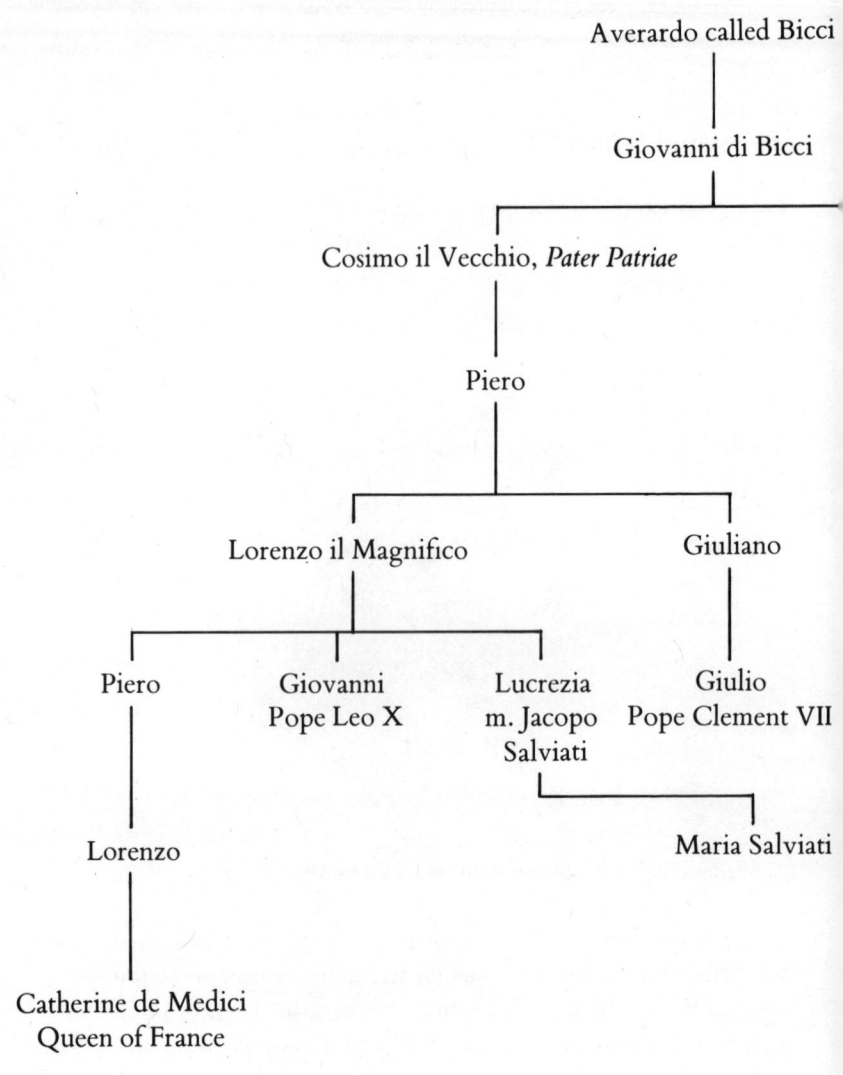

Genealogical Table of the Medicis (simplified)

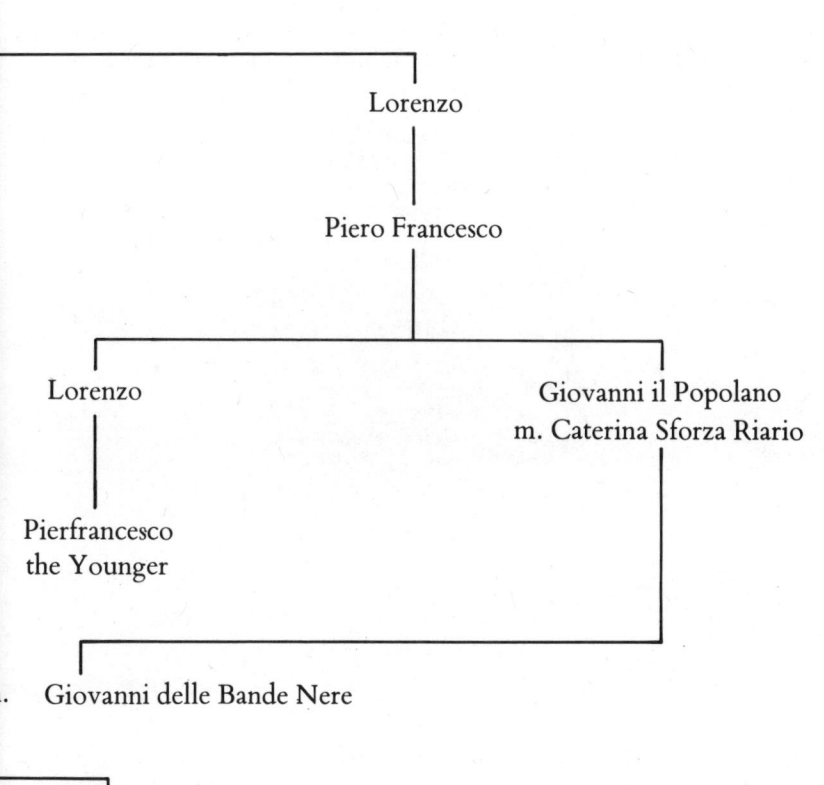

dating from the twelfth century, already existed, and had no doubt been rebuilt as a look-out post by the early Florentine Republic: it was situated on the site of a still older fortified dwelling. The surrounding woods abounded in game of all kinds, and for Cosimo it was a perfect retreat in the heat of summer, as well as a hunting lodge.

The architect was the famous Renaissance Florentine, Michelozzo Michelozzi, and the architecture is of great interest. Built against two sides of the tower, and starting from an outside

Lorenzo il Magnifico.

staircase in the small courtyard, the levels of the main building proceed upwards in stages round the court.

The Medici were a Florentine family, originating in all likelihood from the Mugello, and possibly from a still extant thirteenth-century house at Campiano near Cafaggiolo. As for the derivation of their name, the least romantic explanation is the one most likely to be correct—that they were probably apothecaries or doctors, because *medico* is Italian for doctor, and therefore the famous 'balls' of the coat of arms were originally pills. The branch of the family which concerns this narrative descended from

Giovanni di Bicci, Cosimo's father. The senior branch ended with Catherine de Medici, who became Queen of France, while the cadet branch, descended from Cosimo's younger brother Lorenzo, became the Grand Dukes of Tuscany.

Cosimo, his son Piero and his grandchildren must have spent many happy days hawking over the hills, hunting with dogs, and fishing in the river Sieve. Their actual summer base, and their favourite country retreat, was the old castle of Cafaggiolo, which was rebuilt rather later than Il Trebbio, in about the year 1450, also by Michelozzo. But at the death in 1492 of Lorenzo il Magnifico, Cosimo's grandson, the Florentines rejected the authority of his son Piero—known to history as 'Piero the Unfortunate'—and the Medicis were exiled from Florence.

For the next century and a half Il Trebbio remained the property of the family, though they rarely visited it. Around the year 1650 it was sold to a Florentine merchant, who, however, died not long afterwards.

He left the property to the religious order of the Filippini, with the proviso that a church should be built in his memory. Thus it was that the big church of San Filippo Neri in Florence (known today as San Firenze), together with the lovely oratory adjoining it, was built between the Bargello and the Palazzo della Signoria, taking about one hundred years to complete. And so it befell that for more than two hundred years the *castello* became a religious haven, echoing the orisons of monks and priests who must frequently have paced the pergola, their eyes fixed on their breviaries. Did they, I wonder, ever think of their Medicean predecessors, who had so blithely aired their somewhat heretical views, up and down in the shade of that self-same pergola?

The Filippini Fathers ran the property with success, and detailed accounts and carefully coloured plans of all the *poderi*, or peasant farms, can still be viewed in the Uffizi archives. Many of the old peasant family Renaissance names were in existence right up to the dissolution of the *mezzadria* system of agriculture after the second world war.

Towards the end of the nineteenth century Il Trebbio once more changed hands, and was badly neglected by its new owner. In 1882, however, it was acquired by Prince Mancantonio Borghese, Duke of Bomarzo, who already owned Cafaggiolo. He did much to put the property into order, planting young oak trees and reorganizing the *poderi*, but as the family lived at Cafaggiolo Il Trebbio was allowed to fall into ruins, except for the rooms in the tower. After two generations the whole estate came once more on to the market, and thus it was that my husband bought both *castelli*, intending to use Il Trebbio as our 'country cottage'.

Neglected and half-ruined (from one point on the first floor it was possible to look through to the sky), and surrounded by an impenetrable fence of brambles, brushwood and nettles, the task of restoring it to a habitable dwelling seemed to me hopeless. But Enrico had the vision and the courage to start at once on restoration, and many of the local population found welcome work. There was a wonderful family of stone-masons—indeed, art was in their hands and minds, and I still often admire the beauty of our walls and pavings. The old quarry, one kilometre to the south, was rediscovered under stunted trees and scrub, and the beautiful cream-coloured stone was fashioned into suitable shapes and sizes and loaded on to low, small-wheeled farm-carts drawn by lovely white long-horned oxen, who dragged their loads towards the *castello*, aided by shouts and a small whip, up the last steep slope to the base of the tower.

The methods followed in the restoration were almost identical with those used by the original builders: the wooden scaffolding lashed with rope, the ladders, the ropes, pulleys and buckets, the hand-mixed cement, the long-handled shovels, the paper caps of the workmen, and, perhaps, the pleasure with which they carried out their tasks. I remember the loving care of one of those excellent stone-masons, as he chipped a circular ball by eye, with the aid of a hand-compass, till it was smooth and completed to his satisfaction. The grooved paving-stones of the court and the solid stone balustrade of the open stairway were all hand-worked. Each one of the huge new beams for the roof and the little wooden slats beneath the humped tiles had to be made as nearly as possible to resemble the original. All the windows were of small leaded panes of casement glass, and the chimneys which were added were of fifteenth-century design. The derelict farm buildings against the south side were demolished to make way for a terrace garden, and the scrub cleared for a lawn surrounded by age-old cypress trees. It was a joyous new beginning. The chapel on the piazza was also restored: it is of perfect proportions, and except for the outer walls was entirely designed by Michelozzo; it is a small gem of vaulted ecclesiastical architecture. The altarpiece of the 'Madonna and Six Saints', now in the Accademia of Florence, came from here.

The work went on nearly all that summer of 1937 while we lived there with only a few rooms sparsely furnished. The redesigned ceilings were painted by a small artisan named Bellioni, grey-haired, round-faced and gay, peeping over his metal-rimmed spectacles under a black beret and repeating 'Già, già'—meaning 'yes, yes' or 'I see'—when consulted in his work; he wore a dark

grey overall and grubby white sneakers, for he was up and down ladders or scaffolding all day long, carrying to and fro an old kerosene can with a rope handle in which he mixed his paints for the stencils and the hand-work in the execution of the new painted wooden ceilings. The designs we followed were a mixture of the colourless traces found under the old whitewash of the walls and (the majority) of patterns taken from ceilings in Florence and adapted to our needs. There was one original ceiling which needed little repair, but the woodwork of nearly all the others had to be replaced.

We were fortunate in having a very good iron-worker at the forge at Cafaggiolo who made us excellent copies of old doorhandles, hinges, locks and bolts. The carpentry work was also excellent for most of the doors and window-frames, but the heavier doors, with embossed panels of beautifully grained chestnut wood, were made in Siena, including the heavy arched double entrance door. The well-head was acquired in Arezzo.

Watching those industrious workmen swarming up and down the rope-lashed wooden scaffolding, I pictured the much earlier times of the original building, and the still earlier days when Cosimo and his architect friend Michelozzo Michelozzi came to inspect the site. Only the tower then stood, roofless on the little rocky promontory where, at that time, there were no cypress trees, but some oaks and scrub. I could picture Cosimo quite clearly, spare of frame, dark of complexion and rather gaunt of aspect. His companion and friend was stockier of build and rounder of face, with a bushy beard. These two men, as I 'saw' them, had probably ridden up from Cafaggiolo, which, though already a Medici property, was still a mediaeval fortress complete with moat and drawbridge. I pictured Cosimo taking his ease on the slope below the *castello* which would become the kitchen garden, enjoying one of his rare moments of relaxation as he looked down and across the Mugello plain to the birthplace of Fra Angelico and also to that of Giotto, who must have been a great source of inspiration to Cosimo in all his work of rebuilding in Florence.

The vision of these original builders faded, but the shovelling, the chipping and the hammering continued towards the complete restoration of this masterpiece of domestic architecture. The garden, too, was taking shape: the walling, the paved paths, the planting of the box hedges, the rose garden, the gravelled entrance-way, the water troughs and the planting of the grass. All this was practically completed in less than a year, and at times we had as many as sixty or seventy men employed in the enterprise.

With the property went forty farmsteads, sixteen at Cafaggiolo and the rest, mainly hill-farms, at Il Trebbio. The administration, the huge granary and the main wine cellars were all at Cafaggiolo, and I was told that more than four hundred people lived on the estate.

At that time the traditional *mezzadria* system of agriculture still prevailed—an equal sharing of all the main produce between the owner and the farmer (known as a *capoccia*). He and his family, including the older children, worked an intensive cultivation of wheat and oats, maize, vines and olives, and they also raised beans, potatoes, tomatoes and the like. They normally kept a pair of long-horned white oxen, and often a pair of *vacche*, their short-horned female counterparts, a few sheep, a pig and some poultry. The cattle and the livestock were actually the property of the landlord, who was responsible for buying them, though after the war they were shared with the farmer, who, if an animal died, paid for half the cost of its replacement.

The good peasant farmer left no corner of his land uncultivated, and fruit trees—apple, cherry, pear or fig—were dotted here and there in the open, undulating fields. Though the *mezzadria* system had changed in many ways during the last hundred years in favour of the farmer, the way of life still remained rather feudal, and the last vestiges of the rights of the landlord were apparent in the almost daily arrival at our back door (we had one in those days) of a child or some other member of a peasant family with a few eggs or whey-cheese, a basket of fruit in season, or, rarely, a scraggy chicken, for all of which the bringer was awarded a few *soldi*. The wiles of the farmer also remained, to cheat the *padrone* and, if he could, the agent, or *fattore*. It was all a recognized sort of game; but if the proprietor was smart enough not to be misled he was usually respected, and occasionally even liked.

The farmers paid no rent, and could, with their consent, be moved from one farm to another according to the acreage to be worked and the size of the family. The *padrone* had all the responsibility, except for casual repairs, but gave no wages, and the agent's office at Cafaggiolo was like a small bank operated on the debit and credit system.

This method of working the land had been in practice for hundreds of years, originating in Roman times. After the emancipation of the peasants from the time of the rise of the Florentine republic in the thirteenth century it worked very well indeed, when much of the city's food supply came from the Mugello. In some cases, where the peasant was an indifferent worker and was in debt to the *padrone*, he could be dismissed (and he always had the right to leave if he wished), but this was not usual unless he had committed some crime such as continued poaching or threshing grain clandestinely.

Within his domain the *padrone*'s word was law, even in the immediate post-war days of social change. I remember so well when Enrico, who was in Rome at the time, asked me to hold a Mass for his mother a month after she had died. The appointed day fell on a Sunday, and we duly had the funeral service—black drapes and all over a fictitious coffin—but no one, not even the officiating priest, considered it seemly to tell me that a Mass in suffrage could not be held on a Sunday, the Lord's day. . . .

Summers became a joy spent at Il Trebbio with Virginia, our fair-haired little daughter, and our son. There was great rejoicing when Lorenzo was born. The local population staged an impromptu dance on the main road and in front of the *castello*, and Alfredino Aiazzi, a young man from the village, sat on the low wall by the roadside playing the accordion while all and sundry danced. A carload of tourists who had just put behind them all the interminable bends of the road over the Apennines from Bologna were held up by this unexpected scene. They asked what it was all about, and were told, '*È nato un padroncino*'—'A little *padrone* has been born'. That evening there were flares all round the roofed embrasures of Cafaggiolo and Il Trebbio.

I loved the light patches of the fruit-tree blossoms in relief against the emerald green of the young wheat or oats or barley; the looped-up vines within the neat rows of little supporting trees alternating with the wide strips of the planted grain, and the tender green of the first wrinkled vine-shoots in leaf against the dark twisted stems of the vines themselves; the cry of 'Heu-yah!' from the peasant behind the yoked oxen as he prepared the ground for the planting of the maize; the whirr of the pheasant's wing flushed from her nest of olive brown eggs; the whistling warble of the little siskins darting among the undergrowth and the lovely song of the blackcap, resembling that of the nightingale—all this at our doorstep, and away beyond, as a back-drop, the blue haze over the Mugello plain, culminating in the broken line of the Apennine range of mountains.

The harvesting in July of the staple crop of maize was gay with the orange corn-cobs, stripped of their crackling, paper-like sheaths and drying in the hot summer sun on the paved open yards of the farms. As the sun sank behind the western hills the rays caught the humped-tiled roofs and the walls of the houses, enhancing their colours.

The big yearly event was the threshing of the grain, when each farm in turn was visited by the cumbersome, box-like wooden contraption which was the threshing machine. It was hauled up our hill by six of the long-horned oxen, and all the neighbours gathered in turn to speed the work. It was a tiring and a dusty task in the heat of July and August. All the chaff had to be carried away in large round open baskets and the straw had to be stacked. There were always bets between the *capoccia* and the *fattore* as to the total weight of the wheat harvested. Gargantuan meals were, of course, part of the ritual, and at dusk we often heard the pad of hooves and the rattle of the cart-wheels as the sacks of grain went down to the capacious granary at Cafaggiolo.

Spring and autumn saw the big white oxen yoked to the plough, which in those days was made with a good blade of iron, though even as late as the last century it had still been made of wood with a metal tip to form the furrow. 'Heu-yah!' shouted the peasant, and the obedient beasts strained slowly forward. 'Ssss–ah!' hissed the man, and the oxen willingly stopped, blowing through their black nostrils as they waited for the next word of command. Then some other member of the family turned the unwieldy team in their tracks—'Heu-yah!'—and again they responded. These sounds echoed across the hillside as they had done for hundreds of years.

There were other sounds, too, those of the axe and the saw, and the bleat of the sheep as the children herded them back to their pens at dusk, the tinkle of the bells round the necks of a few, and those of a deeper tone attached to some of the cattle also on their way home from pasturing in the woods. In the spring there came the cry of a cock pheasant going to roost, with all the other farmyard noises of reluctant animals and birds being herded in for the night.

The vintage was perhaps the happiest time, for wine is so universally enjoyed. All the families were out in the fields in the first days of October, snipping the dark bunches of grapes with kerchief or hat well over the face to avoid the earwigs and other insects which infested the fruit, and dropping them into baskets or into the high, small wooden tubs, which in their turn were loaded on to the carts drawn by the white *vacche*, and then emptied into the large, open wooden vats and trodden down underfoot. Later the juice was transferred to the big closed barrels for fermenting. Each family drank their own wine.

The olive harvest, in winter, was rather different. The olives were first ground under two huge upright granite millstones revolving in a large metal trough. In our day this process was already being carried out by electric power. The crushed olives were put into porous rope containers and stacked under an iron press, from which the oil filtered through into a trough below the floor. The press was worked by an unwieldy but ingenious device and the simultaneous effort of three stalwart men.

The visiting charcoal burners camping in the woods always seemed a little mysterious. Their large, flat, round ovens were built of short sticks of chestnut wood stacked compactly and upright, and then entirely covered with turf. The fire took several days to penetrate all through, and from the centre arose a thin column of smoke above the trees.

The mule-train, owned by a grand rustic from the Abruzzi, by name Rinaldo, often stopped to graze on our piazza, or we heard the pad and shuffle of hooves as the good beasts, roped head to tail, went up or down our hill on their mission of fetching and carrying the charcoal or loads of wood. To our sorrow the charcoal-burners did not return after the war, though Rinaldo and his beguiling mule-train are still with us.

CHAPTER II

THE PLEASANT WINTERS in Rome and the summers in our Tuscan paradise allowed us sometimes to forget the uneasy present and steep ourselves in the past. I learned of the many celebrities who had been connected with the land of the Mugello, of times long since faded almost into legend, and of the many Medici who came and went their way.

The Countess Matilde of Canossa, the last ruler of a much larger Tuscany, had had a villa at nearby San Piero a Sieve, and had been a friend of Archbishop Anselm of Canterbury in the twelfth century. St Francis of Assisi founded a monastery which is visible from our cypress-lined terrace. The exiled Thomas à Becket is reputed to have dedicated the church of San Bartolomeo at San Galliano, then recently restored, in the year 1163, and left a beautifully worked cope and a chalice as a gift. Part of the house where Giotto was born is still standing, while the birthplace of Fra Angelico is at Vocchio, in the southern Mugello. Giotto was much patronized by Cosimo de Medici, who had a special interest in this district, the homeland of his family.

Then there was the famous Contessa Caterina Sforza Riario, who defended her estates beyond the Apennines against the diabolical Cesare Borgia with fantastic courage; she visited Il Trebbio when she was contesting the right of inheritance of her infant son Giovanni de Medici. This child became a ruthless *condottiero*, though his military exploits were admired by the Florentines. The worldly Cardinal Carlo de Medici, brother of one of the Grand Dukes of Tuscany, was passionately fond of hunting, and the ducal court was often at Cafaggiolo, so I expect the Cardinal arranged grand gatherings at Trebbio after the chase, which no doubt he followed on his mule—preferred in those days to a horse.

Nevertheless, behind these happy beginnings at Trebbio the clouds of war were gathering. Mussolini had now been dictator for sixteen years, though King Vittorio Emanuele was still on the throne. Il Duce, who had started his career as a socialist journalist in central Italy, had been raised to power by the King in October

The Cardinal Carlo de Medici

1922, after the famous March on Rome by the recently constituted Fascist Party, in the hope that he would be able to put an end to the disorder and violence resulting from the first world war. He had immature and lamentable ideas of national aggrandizement (he actually attempted to revive the Roman Empire), and loved to appear as a strong man of the people—whenever possible with nude torso—but he never went too near a battle, and avoided armed clashes. He was no ogre, but as he grew older he suffered from megalomania and preferred to have only 'yes-men' around him.

Though he was not a statesman, nevertheless, with all his faults and the eventual irreparable havoc that he wrought, he can be remembered with gratitude for his achievements in improving so greatly the roads, railways, hospitals and schools, and above all the health and physique of the people, more especially of the rising generation through his schemes for school milk and gymnastics. He did much for the Italians.

A dictator has been likened to a man on a bicycle: if he stops he falls off. So Mussolini prepared a colonial enterprise aimed at the military occupation of Eritrea. It was not unpopular among the people, who felt that if it was successful it would erase memories of the blow to national pride when the Eritreans had defeated the Italians at Adowa at the end of the last century. But the Duce had failed to gauge the extent of international opposition to his plan. Even so, rather than draw back his army he preferred to launch Italy into the seemingly impossible conquest of Abyssinia. When, unexpectedly, the Italians were victorious, the Duce was acclaimed by his deluded people as a great conqueror, and they were glad to be able to think of themselves as eventual colonial benefactors of the backward Abyssinian peoples. Mussolini was by this time already aping the tactics of Adolf Hitler and beginning to regard himself as invincible. Nevertheless, these bellicose activities, followed by the complicated intervention in the Spanish Civil War, left the Italian economy in a very parlous state.

The outbreak of war in 1939, beginning with the invasion of Poland by the Germans and Russians, was for Italy, not yet involved in the hostilities, a time of terrible apprehension and suspense. Anxiety deepened into impenetrable gloom when Mussolini declared war on France and England on June 10th, 1940. He did not consult his Fascist Grand Council, the King, or even his German allies. Hitler was furious, and it would seem that he never trusted the Duce again. Nor had Mussolini any trust in Hitler.

On that June day the people remained incredulous but passive. There was a general feeling that something might still happen to prevent such a disaster as war: the King could threaten to abdicate—he could abdicate—he could make an alliance with the Pope—His Holiness himself could denounce the Government. The people looked helplessly for a lead which was not there, a salvation which was never really a possibility to save them not only from the horrors of war, but from disgrace in the eyes of civilized nations. The political ground had been too well prepared; the people's gods had feet of clay.

As for Enrico and myself, something seemed to die in us when my husband called out the terrible news (which he had heard on the radio) from an upper window as I worked in the rose garden, for we both remembered so well the 1914–1918 war. For something to do we took the car down to get petrol at the single pump on the main road not far from where the people of Cafaggiolo had danced in celebration of Lorenzo's birth. The old woman who worked the pump wore her usual expression of fatalistic unconcern. We spoke of the terrible news, but she only said, as she rocked the pump handle to and fro, '*Bè-an-che-ques-to-pas-ser-à*' ('Well, this too will pass'), accentuating each syllable with the rhythmic to-and-fro movement of the handle.

Later, when war became a reality, the great majority of the population remained dumbly hostile, for to be told that the British, and later the Americans, were now enemies just made no sense at all. For centuries the German-speaking people had been the hereditary foe. The only general interest was concentrated on the effort to prevent, whenever possible, the menfolk from being absorbed into the army and sent out of the country. All manner of means were employed to this end. Our gardener, for instance, who had been called up three or four times, had a successful technique for faking asthma, and he became so competent at the deception that he ended by contracting the affliction. He blithely admitted that he had no courage: '*Non sono coraggioso io!*'

Our rural summers continued remote from war, with the lack of transport affecting us little, for we were almost entirely self-supporting. We shared our good fortune with a family of evacuated children who were, before very long, wearing home-spun woollen garments because a few of the older women had unearthed old-fashioned spinning wheels. Almost the only daily commodity missing was salt. Our home-produced wine was the remedy, or at least the consolation, for much distress and the lack of news from the absent menfolk. The increased farm-work was tiring, and there was the uncertainty whether any of the parcels, so lovingly despatched, ever reached their destination. But the *santa pazienza* carried the people along; the sun shone, and after the wheat harvest the maize ripened in almost tropical heat. The war, in fact, was like the skeleton in the cupboard or a menacing cloud overhead: it seemed to have little contact with our daily lives. This feeling of futility was increased by the absence of any war-work, for there was no mobilization of civilians. In fact, there was no national war effort at all—not even the collection of waste materials; each did what they could, in one way or another, for their own relatives, friends or dependants.

For reliable news the more educated listened to the foreign broadcasts, but these were not hopeful, and depression was national (except for the few exuberant Fascists). The press continued to publish news of victories and the Duce to make speeches from the balcony of the Palazzo Venezia in Rome, endeavouring to revive the flagging enthusiasm for the glorious Fascist cause. Nevertheless, by the end of 1942 it was evident that the Nazi–Fascist entente was facing eventual defeat.

Then, in the summer of 1943, Mussolini was dramatically deposed. Dino Grandi, formerly Italian ambassador to London, led the revolt at the last Grand Council at the Palazzo Venezia. That August the Allies landed first in Sicily and then on the beaches at Salerno and Naples. Field-Marshal Badoglio was made head of a provisional government, and managed to conclude an armistice with the Allies, but without advising the Germans.

That day the people of the Mugello went wild with joy, as if there had been an overwhelming victory, downing tools and celebrating the event. The Allies were never again so popular. But after barely a day of confused jubilation the Germans invaded Italy in strength, relentlessly crushing our ill-timed rejoicing. The news came through to us at Il Trebbio that they were only a few miles distant, crossing the Apennines and speeding southwards. On the spur of the moment I decided—since Enrico was in Rome—to send the children up to one of the outlying hill farms.

The excitement of such an adventure was quite to the liking of the young, who, happy and without fear, greatly enjoyed the expedition: the lighted courtyard, the patient oxen with the carts piled high with bedding, the bags of food, cooking pots, a lamp and other necessities, the general hustle and confusion, and finally the long, slow trek up the hill by full moonlight in the balmy air of a summer's night—and so at last, exhausted, they fell asleep on the floor of the rural homestead, in the thrilling proximity of rabbits, kittens, chickens, other children, and a tame jay with no tail which lived in the peasant's kitchen.

Luckily the precaution proved unnecessary, for the Germans kept strictly to the main roads, but as I lay in bed that night I could not sleep. I listened in agony to the heavy and incessant rumble of the armoured vehicles, a noise that continued by day as well as by night, as guns, tanks and other fearful machines bore down to the Salerno front, where the Allies were fighting to retain and extend their foothold on the beaches south of Naples.

However, the frightened populace, after fleeing from their homes on the main roads, cautiously returned when they found that they would remain unmolested. There must have been many other times of enforced flight all through the ages when local wars were not uncommon. The soldiery of those days were almost invariably rapacious, merciless and cruel, and in comparison the European armies of today are models of virtue.

The Mugello has always seemed to attract these mercenaries, from Hannibal's hordes (there is still an old Roman bridge bearing his name), through the terrifying Galli and the various invasions of the Goths, right down to the much smaller armies of local warring states. There was even an Englishman, Sir John Hawkwood, who fought for the Florentines against Pisa, and whose large equestrian portrait can be seen, frescoed by Paolo Uccello, on the left-hand wall of the cathedral in Florence.

The Allied bombing began from bases established in the south of Italy, and sometimes the bombs fell in unexpected places. One glorious summer morning the *castello* was shaken by such a fierce explosion and blast that it seemed as though an air battle had suddenly been let loose above our heads. We were stunned by surprise and uncertainty as we herded the children into the cellar. Later we found that some forty bombs had been dropped below us two kilometres away, probably unloaded by planes returning from a bombing raid on Spezia. They fell near the railway line in the valley, and, situated as we were on the hill, the upward blast caught us with a force which seemed quite uncanny. These air formations came over quite frequently, flying high northwards to their targets, and there was no defence—nor could there be any.

Then began the passage southwards of many escaped conscripts and prisoners of war, for most of the camps had been opened on the day of the armistice, the gaolers probably delighted to be free of their charges. At other camps the Italians, having no orders, just allowed the prisoners to walk out unimpeded.

Of the fifty or sixty thousand prisoners who were at large all over the country, the great majority tried to work their way south to the Allied lines. A few were successful, but most of them were wandering about or hiding in central Italy. In pairs or groups these homeless men found homes, assistance or even work on their endless journeying, and many are the treasured scraps of paper thanking the Italians for help received.

Our first two fugitives took us off-guard. They were English officers, and because we had been warned of the dire penalties promised for those harbouring escaped prisoners we failed to help them as we wanted to. Subsequently we spent fruitless time searching the woods calling to the dog in English to try to attract their attention. After this failure we devised a good plan of action: while appearing to upbraid the fugitives in loud tones, we managed to tell them where to hide, and subsequently, during the inevitable hours of the siesta or in the evening, supplied them not only with food but with such precious utilities as candles, matches, knives, maps, bandages, pencils, paper and string, and sometimes with mugs of tea from clandestine supplies. The majority were South Africans taken prisoner in the North African campaign, but there were also English, Scots, a few Americans, and one Irish Free State parachutist. The most difficult to deal with were those who arrived still in uniform, but these were few, though the particular need for footwear was sometimes a problem, since army boots were easily recognizable.

Sometimes these vagrant ex-prisoners were recaptured, loaded on to cattle-trucks and despatched by rail northwards. Their method of escape in these circumstances was to squeeze through the ventilator, and when the train was travelling very slowly, or was stationary—which was not uncommon in the existing state of the railways—they dropped down between the carriages and lay flat on the tracks until the train had passed.

In the first days of the passage of these vagrants we were rather too generous, so that eventually we had little left to give, after our ski-ing clothes (my own clothing was gladly accepted by the smaller men) had been distributed. Our 'visitors' turned up with great regularity—they usually came in twos or threes—and so our activities were inevitably known, though all the peasants helped them too, for were they not all beloved sons of some anxious mother at home? We were obviously on one of those grapevine routes indicated by circumstances. Most of them, after leaving us, found their way to a village near Fiesole above Florence, where the whole population was anxious to help them: none the less, it all became a bit dangerous. Travelling by train was also by now rather precarious, and Enrico found it increasingly difficult to reach us from Rome. We knew that, for the ordinary citizen, it might soon be impossible to get about at all. The Allied armies were slowly advancing towards the capital, and we felt that it might be unwise to have the family divided for an unforeseeable period, so it was decided that we should attempt to join Enrico in Rome as soon as possible.

We arranged for the *castello* to be occupied by the Sisters of Charity who ran an orphanage at Cafaggiolo, and they were happy to agree to our proposal. We acquired a car to take us to Florence, and set out on October 21st, 1943.

CHAPTER III

OUR MISTAKE WAS to travel in a bunch, ten of us. The party consisted of our friend Diana Corsi, with her children of five and two, myself, Virginia and Lorenzo, Kate Presbitero, an elderly artist friend, our nursemaid, and Pietro, our servant.

The journey to Florence was comparatively easy, but once there the difficulties began. Lodgings were almost unprocurable, and our rooms, booked in advance, had been given away to others, so we had to make do with a room with two beds for the children and myself, while Kate had a shake-down behind a screen in the passage outside. The Corsi family found a room in a remote *pensione*, where they spent a sleepless night trying to eliminate existing 'tenants'.

Our intention to leave the next morning by train was frustrated, as the permit for our heavy luggage was not forthcoming (it contained little but contraband provisions), and also because the line to Rome was blocked—a familiar occurrence. So Wednesday passed in cajoling and planning. The curfew ended at 5 a.m., and we managed to get a cab to come and take us to the station the next morning, risking the line being open.

In the early hours, while it was still dark, we arrived at the station and met the Corsis, who had come on foot. For the next two and a half hours we waited for the train, sitting among crowds of exhausted people who, by their appearance, seemed to have been there for days. We were then joined by a travel agent dressed in brilliant blue and gold, and the crowds began to eye us with suspicion. Summoned by this apparition, we followed him into a glass-walled office, into which the people continued to stare vacantly. At 7.30 we were taken on to the platform, and held ourselves ready to storm the incoming train. By dint of much 'largesse' we secured the corridor flap-seats in the only wagon-lit. We left Paolo, the chauffeur, to follow as best he could, accompanying the 'contraband' luggage.

At midday we arrived in Chiusi, halfway between Florence and Rome. Here we were greeted by air-raid alarms, and the information that the big railway viaduct just north of Orvieto was down. So we had the choice of staying at Chiusi station, or of returning to Florence by the train that had brought us. Having got so far, we decided to try to go on, and lowered our unwieldy party on to the railway track. Chiusi, which was one of the main distribution stations for the railway's electric supply, was an inevitable bombing target—as yet unbombed—and Germans in uniform swarmed everywhere.

The psychological effect on people suddenly flotsamed and as yet unaccustomed to insecurity was interesting. They wandered about anxiously, accosting strangers as though they were their only hope of salvation, either bewildered or indignant. A very young mother with her infant in arms sat forlornly on her luggage in the station square, while her equally young husband asked all his neighbours for help or advice, almost weeping in his anxiety. A lady's maid from north Italy, returning to her mistress in Rome, hurriedly tried to tell me her life history, somehow feeling that because her 'lady' was English we could all join up; anything to feel less abandoned, to achieve some kind of plan for the morrow. Some of the travellers were packed off to Viterbo in rickety-looking trucks or equally unreliable cars: the fare had to be paid in advance, with no guarantee of arrival, and there was an even chance that the cars might be commandeered by the Germans en route.

I got in touch with friends living nearby, who luckily were able to give us beds. The Corsis and Kate were less fortunate, for all I could find for them was the Hotel d'Italia, of very doubtful cleanliness and with no service and nothing to eat. I forget where Pietro slept, but with his usual resourcefulness he found accommodation somewhere. Mercifully we had brought enough food with us for two days. And so to bed, though the wail of the air-raid alarm all through the night made it difficult to sleep.

The next morning, as no car was available, we decided to return to Florence. We were told that a return train was being made up that afternoon, and Pietro went to the station to arrange about seats and the luggage while we awaited his return. The little Etruscan museum was closed, and we were in no mood to go sightseeing in the famous tombs in the vicinity. There was nothing else of interest except a certain squalid picturesqueness which is common to most of these villages. The irregular dark grey, sometimes almost black, stone houses were clustered together, presenting their backs to the hilly Umbrian landscape; sometimes they were festooned with lines of scanty washing. Inside these erstwhile strongholds there are often enchanting little squares where the friendly inhabitants cluster about the main fountain. But in Chiusi there reigned a sordid gloom, and the inhabitants were, as we say, *antipatico* or even hostile, so it was with relief that we made our way to the edge of the town, which is perched on a ridge, and found seats on a wide terrace overlooking the valley. We had been told that the local bus was still running, and that if we waited there it might possibly take us further on our journey.

It was very hot, and passing German military traffic covered us with dust. One hour later, when most certainly the train to Florence had left, we learned that the bus had been commandeered to take refugee women and children to Rome! Despairing and shamefaced, we returned to the lodgings we had occupied before, and I dared not tell Diana or Kate that should any Germans arrive, whatever the hour, they would be turned out of their beds and into the corridors.

Pietro telephoned from the station, which is some distance from the town, with the news that another consignment of refugees might be despatched to Rome the following day. Diana and I raced down the hill in the fading light and contacted all visible authority, but learned nothing except that there was a possibility of another bus leaving the next morning at eight. With difficulty and a gift of persuasion born of desperation I got my hostess to persuade her *fattore* to cajole a peasant to produce a bullock-cart which would take us to the station. So at dawn the party descended into the valley behind the leisurely white oxen, the children on the straw at the bottom of the cart and Kate perched on a kitchen chair. On the station square we formed quite an artistic refugee group, arranged to catch the eye of some more chivalrously minded official should one be near; and so we waited through air-raid alarms, either for a bomb or for a bus. Men were loaded on to trucks and disappeared to some unknown destination in a whirl of dust, but there seemed to be just as many people as before.

At 9.30 the bus actually materialized, closed, comfy and solid, and we stormed it together with a crowd of screaming and kicking women. The children survived, and we got seats near the front. We waved to Pietro, who had loaded our suitcases on the roof, supposing that he would follow when and how he could. With relief we moved off, and only later learned that our destination was Orvieto, which is about halfway between Chiusi and Rome. The weather, however, was heavenly, and the German driver and conductor kind and patient with the women on board—most of them, it seemed, black-market traffickers.

Later, when we stopped at the urgent request of the children, we caught sight of Pietro on the roof with the luggage. The Germans wanted to remove him, but I explained his relationship to us and they let him remain.

We arrived at Orvieto at midday and were dumped with our belongings in the town square. There was a rumour that the railway to Rome might be open again the next day, and in the meantime we managed to find a pleasant hotel, just beyond the archway on the piazza, and have a happy 'family' luncheon party posing (not very convincingly) as *la bella famiglia italiana*—grandmama, daughter, daughter-in-law and grandchildren. Orvieto is a lovely town, but we were too preoccupied to enjoy it, except of course in contrast to Chiusi. Accommodation was not difficult, and we found comfortable rooms and slept reasonably well, despite air-raid alarms.

In the afternoon I went down to the German High Command, quartered in a fine building on the edge of the town—which is, as always, built on a hill—hoping for transport or at least to get news through to Enrico in Rome. The Italian sentries let me pass, but a little further on a Fascist militia officer was very dubious about my mission, but did refer me to a superior officer. I gained audience with this German major, and waited while he busily talked and argued with members of his staff about transport and petrol problems. Almost dozing in my fatigue, a sudden and staccato '*Und jetzt Ihnen?*' brought me in a sort of panic to attention, and I explained my mission with suitable humility.

The major was typically curt and tight in speech and figure, the Prussian officer, civil but not very helpful; there were no private cars, of course, and we should do best to take our chance on a half-empty truck departing from the town square. (A bus for Rome had, incidentally, left that very morning, empty.) I explained very earnestly, in my best but nevertheless indifferent German, that my aged aunt had a weak heart, the children were small, we were tired—in fact, exhausted—and we had been travelling for days. '*Wir können nichts mehr.*' The major hesitated, and then sent me off with a sergeant whose office, in which there were several other non-coms, was not so formal or exalted. It had a wonderful view north in which he pointed out to me the bombed viaduct that had caused our débâcle at Chiusi. Presently a colonel came in, the non-commissioned officers sprang to attention, and I was asked again to tell my pathetic story of travel and strain, the old and the helpless dependent on the chivalry, etc., etc. . . . He asked me to wait. The fact that I was English, even though married to an Italian, seemed to worry him not at all—nor, for that matter, any of the other Germans who helped us on our way.

As I waited, I found that the German sergeant was rather a wag, though I could not follow all his back-chat with the other non-coms, who came and went, so I reverted to the contemplation of the broken viaduct. Suddenly the colonel returned with another man, a Viennese colonel, who I found was the possessor of a large car which was going to Rome immediately. I thanked everyone fervently, and almost embracing the newly-found saviour hurried off with him in the huge military car, fearing that the children might have disappeared or that Kate might have gone to bed. Luck was with us; I found Virginia and Lorenzo just outside the hotel in the company of an unknown female who claimed to be a member of our party, as she had taken charge of the children, the Corsis having loaded themselves on to a truck full of landmines which was already on the way to Tor di Quinto near Rome.

Kate was half-undressed and ready to turn in. Wine was ordered for the colonel while we feverishly prepared our bags. In fifteen minutes we were safely in the comfortable car, the unknown blonde included. The car and its owner had just been transferred from the Russian front, which the colonel described as gruesome, and he had been given only one day at home with his wife and children en route.

At Viterbo we lost our way and strayed off the main road to Rome, landing ourselves after dark at Civitavecchia on the coast. A sentinel warned us that Allied planes were overhead, and we proceeded at a slow pace and without headlights. Civitavecchia was a heap of the proverbial rubble—bridges down, anti-invasion defences, and a maze of tank traps. We lost our way again and even our direction, and there was not a human soul of whom to ask our route, nor a cat alive in that deserted place. But there was a moon, and at last we hit the right road. Then the petrol gave out and the contents of the reserve tank proved defective. The Italians often tampered with the tanks, putting in water, and they always gave wrong information if asked the way, so travelling by night was a nightmare for the Germans. At each hill—and there were many—the engine failed and we had to turn the heavy car round by pushing it, laden as it was, and freewheel back some way to refill the cleaned carburettor. The children greatly enjoyed all these interruptions—'*Kinder aussteigen!*', '*Kinder einsteigen!*'. The rest of us were almost too tired to react, or to push the car any more. But the three Germans continued to sweat and toil to bring their cargo of Britishers to Rome.

It was nearly midnight before we arrived, running silently down from Monte Mario into the moonlit city, beautiful but dead. With difficulty we were admitted into our own house, because only the Germans were allowed to be abroad after curfew time, and a knock at the door was the dread of every household. At last our faithful cook Mario popped his head out of the window, and I called out that it was the *Signora Padrona*, with the children.

As we were disentangling ourselves from the car, thanking our Austrian colonel, a figure in a red dressing-gown emerged from our double-doored entrance. It was Enrico who, oblivious of all else in the joy of seeing us again, responded in his usual undemonstrative way, saying in English, 'Is this the proper time of night to come home?'

CHAPTER IV

SO WE WERE plunged into wartime occupied Rome—and how different it was from the life of that city when I had arrived as a bride ten years before. It had then been all red-carpeted, and I had found it very grand when I was pitchforked, inadequately prepared, into the world of dinners and cocktail and bridge parties, but also into a life of domestic ease in the large, high-roomed seventeenth century palazzo in the Piazza Navona.

My first visit to Rome had been in 1931, motoring out from England with my brother Gladwyn, who was taking up his duties as Second Secretary with the British Embassy. I remember very little of the journey, except for the tortuous descent, steep and rather perilous, on the main road from Radicorfani south of Siena, and the romantic approach to the Eternal City through the arches cut in the vast Roman walls, with the heavy studded doors still there against the brickwork but imbedded in the cement of the roadway.

Occupied with his new duties, my brother went off the next morning to the embassy and handed me an invitation card to a cocktail party for that afternoon, suggesting that I should go in his stead. I launched myself bravely into the concourse of chattering glass-holders, and was introduced, by my charming American hostess, to people I had never before met. Having done my social best I made hesitant inquiries about the possibility of a taxi, when I heard a voice, deep and kindly but with a non-English accent, saying in my ear, 'Can I see you home?'. I felt that I should refuse, but this man—to whom I had been introduced, and who was no longer very young—seemed so reliable, and of such exceptionally good looks, that I was glad to accept his offer. So out we went into the dim lamp-lit street. 'Can you drive?' was the next question, and in three seconds I found myself at the wheel of a large two-seater Lancia. The traffic, mercifully, was only a fraction of what it is today, and so we arrived safely at our destination.

The next day Gladwyn and I had been invited to lunch with a friend who lived in a flat overlooking the gardens of the Villa Medici, and there we found that our fellow-guest was my beau of the evening before.

For me, I suppose, it was 'love at first sight', or more accurately at second sight; but for Enrico, who was used to easy conquests, I became the possibility and then the hope of a happy family life. However, that period in Rome was not propitious for courtship, and on the advice of my brother I refused an invitation for luncheon, and a few days later took myself off to Bavaria. There followed a long and unusual correspondence between us—hedging, and yet hoping for the happy solution.

We met again in Rome and in London, both times encountering hazards which defeated progress but which, had we been able to view them dispassionately, were not without their humorous side. A later meeting in Munich was more fortunate. I was studying art at the Kunstgewerbe Schule (Polytechnic) in that city, lodging with a couple of elderly sisters, who were immensely excited when Enrico drove up in his grand car. We spent a happy few days together. I had no art whatever in captivating the opposite sex, but this was actually what appealed to Enrico, who had lived for more than twenty years in a very sophisticated world. I remember his great amusement at my hesitation in accepting a pair of shoes, badly needed, as my means were limited.

Enrico's family came from Biella, a small town in the hills north of Turin. Grandpa Giovanni Scaretti, as a young man, had sought his fortune in Rome in the first half of the nineteenth century. He was a heavily built man, and was noted for his rather choleric temper. One day, when walking in old Rome, he noticed a handsome dark girl seated at an open window of her guardian's home—an Italian Monsignore. Giovanni decided that she should be his wife. By name Carlotta Ponselé, she was of French nationality. She grew into a very portly woman, and, judging by her photo, she had an extremely determined disposition. They reared seven children, the fifth of the family being Oreste, Enrico's father, a kindly man and a devoted parent, who handed on the family banking business to the third generation.

As for me, I came from the kind of family which was known at the turn of the century as the 'landed gentry'. I was born in a large rebuilt Elizabethan house in south Yorkshire in a district known as the Dukeries, and the cost of my coming into the world was £5. Unfortunately my family broke up when I was only four years old. My brother Gladwyn, in his memoirs, has described something of our life there, but he did not tell the amusing anecdote of how he casually described to some quite small friend the possessions of his mother—two lakes, three drives and five gold teeth!

It was in Munich that Enrico and I at last became engaged. My mother's not very ardent opposition was dispelled by that able diplomat Sir Ronald Graham, who had recently left Rome, where he had been ambassador for twelve years. He was a friend of Enrico, who had been his favourite companion on the Roman golf course at the Acqua Santa. So it was all settled; we were married in London in October 1933, and I came to the large, rambling house on the Piazza Navona. No one else lived there except my mother-in-law on the second floor. Ten years later, following our epic refugee journey home, she was still there, but maidless, in self-willed discomfort, and entirely out of tune with her fellow creatures or the troubled times in which we lived.

At the time of our marriage Mussolini was already an ailing man: he was often unapproachable, and tended to try to forget his responsibilities in the arms of his mistress Clara Petacci. He had no advisers, and this precipitated his undoing, for his elder brother Arnaldo, who died in the twenties, had been a good and a restraining influence. When Sir Ronald Graham was recalled in 1932, the Duce lost the only man whose advice he sometimes heeded, and so continued alone on his mistaken political course, for which in any case he was quite unfitted. It is a possibility that if Sir Ronald had been British Representative in the late thirties, the German military alliance might never have existed.

When we returned in the autumn of 1943 the air was charged with all the pent-up distress of the years of the unpopular war.

After Mussolini's enforced resignation in July he had been arrested—or taken into 'protective custody', as it was called—but Field-Marshal Badoglio, appointed head of the provisional government, made a fatal mistake in failing to achieve any workable understanding with the Allies. So the war continued, to the bewilderment of the Italian people, who were celebrating the downfall of Fascism. Badoglio's ill-starred interim government was every day more handicapped by the inevitable and increasing suspicion of the Germans, while the Allies had little confidence in the Italian spokesmen who were trying to negotiate peace terms. Although the latter were acting in good faith, and were almost pathetically anxious to appear in a favourable light vis-à-vis the countries which were still their official enemies, nothing constructive was achieved. The result was complete collapse and the loss of all dignity—which, indeed, was inevitable. Some truly great man might have been able, at much personal risk, to retain some semblance of national integrity; but there was no such man, only those whom twenty years of Fascism had sifted to the forefront, ambitious men who, ultimately, had the destiny of their country thrust upon them in a moment of unprecedented complexity and danger. Afraid and incompetent, they were quite unsuited to their tasks. This the people felt deeply, this trailing of the already mud-bespattered Italy in the gutter, this loss of the last vestiges of self-respect; and so, in despair, they turned against the King, who for them represented at this time all that had served to show up the country as mean and dishonourable.

The next six months seemed like so many years. The Germans were now in charge of Rome, and they started a campaign to subdue and organize the city. They never fully succeeded: the Roman technique of misinformation, feigned collaboration and even bland fraud was quite beyond their comprehension, and to deal with it was beyond their capabilities. The hair's-breadth escapes, the adventures, the fantastic existence of thousands of fugitives in hiding, the heroic and the vile amidst the danger and the want and even the ridiculous—these were all ingredients of the daily lives of the majority of citizens, and with time all this caused the loss to the average Roman of ten to forty pounds of his habitual corpulency, so that few could boast of a well-fitting suit of clothes.

Our house in the centre of old Rome, a large, somewhat

labyrinthine complex with two separate entrances and with easy access to the roof, was, not surprisingly, considered a good refuge by some of the fugitives. These belonged to various categories, and included officers of the Italian army who had discarded their uniforms at the declaration of the armistice on September 8th (a few had actually left them in the Ministry of War, changing there into civilian clothes). The terms of this strange and probably unique armistice, based on the 'unconditional' surrender on which

The Piazza Navona showing the Bernini Fountain with the obelisk.

Churchill insisted, were vague in the extreme: they stated that, though the Italians were no longer fighting the Allies, they were to defend themselves if attacked. By whom? The Germans? Communist guerillas? It was, of course, a totally untenable situation for any officer, and incomprehensible to the rank and file of the army, most of whom were taken prisoner and sent to Germany. Later the Allies sponsored a small new Italian army made up of volunteers who fought well on the Adriatic front, but there were so few of them available.

Thus there was a sudden increase in long-habited inmates of monasteries and religious houses. The newly arrived had to learn to moderate their step, while the Trappist 'recruits' were not expected to speak at all.

The Jews were in the greatest danger, since they were liable for deportation to the concentration camps and death in some Nazi gas-chamber. The wives and families of these persecuted people took refuge in nunneries and other Vatican-owned establishments, and at least one Mother Superior asked two applicants, a mother and her daughter, if they had all their false papers in order.

Then there were the ever-increasing number of youths due for military service call-up. A privileged few were admitted into the Papal Guard, but the many others were a problem, so much so that later a few doting parents actually walled up their sons for safety.

Besides all these there were the countless men hiding in belfries or crypts, private apartments, grottoes, woods or other hideouts near the city, nearly all of them escaped prisoners of war. Most of them were English-speaking, trying to join the Allies, who had by now established a bridgehead at Salerno but were prevented from making further advances by the heroic, desperate defence of the Germans at Cassino. The Vatican did much to assist these men: there is a very illuminating book, *The Scarlet Pimpernel of the Vatican*,* about this unusual activity and the adventures of an Irish Monsignore, and also of an Englishman, the British Representative to the Vatican, Sir d'Arcy Godolfin Osborne (later Duke of Leeds), who, incarcerated in that neutral city state, proved an able ally of the Monsignore, aided by his versatile butler Mr May. Very tall, erect, and direct of speech, people usually found Sir d'Arcy impressive. He managed to steer clear of any censure of the infringement of his diplomatic immunity by always giving the impression that he knew nothing whatever of his man-servant's clandestine activities.

Lastly there were all those who for one reason or another preferred to disappear; these were the many ex-Fascists, a few anti-Fascists, and a number of civil servants who were expected to report to a somewhat chimerical Republican Fascist Government at Verona in the north of the country. This was after Mussolini, transferred to a prison-refuge in the Gran Sasso, the highest point

* *The Scarlet Pimpernel of the Vatican* by J. C. Gallagher (Souvenir Press).

in the Abruzzi mountains, had been 'rescued' by the Germans, who—though he himself had no enthusiasm for the role—hoped to use him as a rallying-point to toughen Fascist resistance to the Allies in the north. Very few of these government officials even attempted to get to Verona, but those who did found no satisfactory offices to which to report, and most of them eventually found their way back again.

By this time the King and all his family, except Prince Umberto of Piedmont, had fled to the south under the protection of the Allies. Here they once again set up their government. There were intermittent scares that hostages would be taken from among the more or less prominent citizens of Rome or those who had been in court circles, and this made many more people flee from their homes, and at least sometimes provided us with amusement, because everyone with exalted social pretensions chatted loudly about the dangers of arrest as they fled to one another's houses, trying to disguise their rather obvious movements in a shroud of mystery. Hiding, in fact, became fashionable. So life grew very complex, and to live within all the emergency laws an impossibility; we nearly all qualified for imprisonment or deportation, and some for the death penalty, which had been extended to those harbouring various kinds of fugitives.

For ourselves, I think we must have been protected in a negative way, because we had had an Austrian governess—a Nazi, inevitably, or she would not have been allowed to work in Italy—in our employ all the war years till the armistice and had never discussed politics with her, or been overtly partisan or anti-Fascist.

Owing to the limitations of transport and the irregularity of the post, much information was passed by telephone, and most households had codes referring to the black market, escaped prisoners and other things. These codes referred to books on an infinite variety of subjects, the size, shape and weight of shoes and boots and repairs thereto, doctors' orders and chemists' receipts. Many of these subterfuges were rather a farce, while others were conducted with intelligence and skill by members of the underground movements, but attempts at secrecy became second nature, for we were all more or less 'criminals' avoiding discovery; indeed, each day that passed uneventfully was in a sense a reprieve.

None the less, we endeavoured to live a normal life, Enrico going off to the office daily on his bicycle. Rome was calm except for nightly intermittent shootings and explosions of unknown origin. On October 26th it was said that the German H.Q. had moved from the south to the north of Rome, and that they were dismantling war plants to transport them to Germany; but we heard so many rumours that it was difficult to sift the false from the true. The days flew past, filled with hurried, tiresome efforts to combat the complications of life: acquiring food, cleaning and mending the children's clothes, getting their shoes mended, discovering a reel of thread in some obscure shop—and so on till the evening. The only practical way of dealing with the situation was always to carry a large bag as we went around Rome—which we usually did because we were taking something somewhere else or fetching something edible. In any case, we never knew when we might not have the chance of acquiring food, which we always had to carry home ourselves for fear of losing it. We had ten or more people to feed, and it was essential that we should try to build up some reserves, for our heavy baggage containing the 'contraband' food was still in Florence.

It was impossible not to become obsessed with thoughts of food: how triumphant I felt when a successful expedition into the *bassifondi*, the underworld, produced 4 lb. of lamb. The butcher was a dark man with a great deal of hair, living in a tiny windowless room off a squalid courtyard. The table for the meat was near the door, in front of the bed. Everyone had to be treated with great politeness, for they had the goods and we needed them. A week or two later I found some excellent chestnuts. On one occasion Enrico went out early and came home with a small turkey—a red-letter day.

November 1st was the *Festa di Ogni Santi e Tutti Morti* (All Saints and All Souls), the day of the dead, when every self-respecting Roman pays a visit to the cemetery with flowers, chrysanthemums being almost the only ones in season. We started early to avoid the crowds, and took a special bus from the Rinascente to the Campo Santo of Verano. Here we saw the damage done to the church of San Lorenzo by the first raid on July 19th. Only two columns were left of the entrance loggia, and the roof and frescoes near the entrance were badly damaged. Other bombs had fallen around the large cemetery but the objective, the main railway, was untouched.

Politically we knew nothing, for all the rumours were difficult, if not impossible, to verify. There seemed to be very few police about, but the force was now organized by the Germans, who did it well. There were plenty of vegetables to be had at a price, and in some cases the Germans had helped by putting goods on the market instead of allowing them to be relegated to the (now almost free) black market. In fact, the whole of Rome's poorest population lived by buying and selling on the black market. Those who did not actually bring bags, cases and sacks of contraband into the town on bicycles, push-carts or aged lorries, or humped on their backs, occupied their time by standing in queues to obtain goods of all kinds, such as salt, cigarettes and matches, and then selling their acquisitions at ten or twenty times the cost price. Because of this, and because so many young men were in hiding, it was impossible to find shop-assistants or office workers, and consequently no one was 'unemployed'. Those who had means tended to support the rest of the population by 'eating their patrimony'. The hardest hit were the lower middle class, clerks and others, who had few financial resources and no wish or opportunity to participate in the pillage of the rich. Servants became fewer and fewer, as many returned to their home towns or villages, either frightened by the raids or at the request of their families. We were fortunate to have our elderly, dedicated people; we were able to do a lot for ourselves, and the heavy entrance doors remained closed.

At last, early in November, the luggage arrived, accompanied by Paolo, the chauffeur. It was marvellous to feel that we had some reserves in the house, especially as the meat vendor had vanished from the squalid room in the *bassifondi*, though there was a rumour that he had transferred himself to the second floor, where I hadn't the courage to follow him. We were very excited when someone promised me some potatoes. . . .

On November 5th four small bombs fell near the Vatican diplomatic quarters, but happily there were no casualties except some broken glass. Our part of Rome remained very quiet, and we had no air raid alarms. Business was by now almost at a standstill, and Enrico was wondering what he could do for his clerks at the bank. He managed to get to a weekly game of bridge, but I rarely visited any of my friends, for the more mouselike one could be the better. In the middle of the Piazza Navona, the famous Bernini fountain, with the obelisk and the four seated statues, was gradually being bricked up to protect it from possible air raid damage: this work had been begun after the July 19th attack, but was temporarily stopped when there was talk of making Rome an open city.

Everyone with pro-Allied sympathies—and this was, of course, the great majority—was depressed, as the cold weather drew on, by the talk that the Germans were holding a 'winter line' on the Cassino across Italy. The situation grew worse, for, come what might, no officers or men had the slightest intention of presenting themselves for military or civil service, despite the orders to do so; but dodging and hiding indefinitely presented nearly insuperable difficulties, especially as supplies were daily getting scarcer. We thought of the thousands of fugitives all over Italy, without overcoats or any means of keeping warm; and we feared, too, the reprisals which might be taken against the families of men who refused to obey the orders to report for service.

There was little traffic, except on the main streets, where every car and lorry seemed to be labelled *polizia*. No Italian traffic police were to be seen, only occasionally a German with a white metal circle on a stick, but these men were quite unaggressive. In the side streets people walked along the middle of the road, since the only traffic to be seen consisted of a few bicycles. The crowds milled aimlessly up and down the streets, especially young people, who seemed to have nothing else to do (how did they have the time, I wondered?). There were no taxis left, only a few cabs with hungry-looking horses, the tariff fixed by arrangement.

On one memorable day in the middle of November we each had an egg for breakfast—the first we had seen since our return to Rome (but they cost about ten times their pre-war price). By now the tiny rations for October had been distributed, but none for November had yet been seen, and meat seemed to be unprocurable, except on the black market. One afternoon, when it was warm and sunny, we took the children for a walk along the Tiber, and felt the benefit, moral and physical. We came across a humble-looking man guarding a small lamb on a patch of grass, and a little farther on another lamb was grazing on the slopes leading down to the gardens of Castel Sant' Angelo. One man was cutting grass and putting it into a bag—perhaps for rabbits at home?

Although by now we continually heard 'enemy' aeroplanes overhead, and sometimes heavy bombing towards the coastal district, our own comparatively peaceful existence continued. But we wondered for how long. The Germans seemed to be passing over to the offensive on the Cassino line, and had taken the island of Leros in the Dodecanese. In Russia they continued in full retreat, a bitter cup for their command. We had come to the conclusion that the German line, far from being a myth, as some people said, was very strong, in some places impregnable. We should, we decided, have to adjust our mentality and settle in for the winter. We had one of the green damask panels removed from the drawing-room, where the children slept, so that a wood-burning terracotta stove could be installed. Enrico cycled off, when he could, to get a round of golf, and generally managed to return with food of some kind—one day 4 lb. of spinach and two eggs, another day 8 lb. of spinach, four eggs and a cheese. We took the children to see *Aïda*—their first opera—which was a great thrill for all of us. (In those uncertain times the performances began at 4 p.m.) Virginia decided that the Aïda was a man dressed as a woman—'Just look at her arms and legs—and how she screams!' The production was very good and Gigli sang, but his voice was not what it used to be.

Every household began to make preparations for the time when the Germans might depart from Rome—which, we heard, they could do in three hours. We knew that in such an eventuality we could expect no gas, light or water, and each family made certain of having some reserves of the last two. For ourselves, we had an Aga cooker and a supply of coke and anthracite, so we were among the lucky ones. Our provisions were holding out well, but we were anxiously awaiting a consignment from Tuscany: it was much overdue, and such cargoes often failed to arrive. It did in fact turn up in the middle of December; but for the thousands of unfed, unclothed, ailing and ill, the prospect of the winter was awful.

The growing population of Rome, and more particularly the youths of the city, were starting to come out in cast-off military wear, some of them in carefully retailored uniforms, others in rags and tatters. Footwear was varied and often pathetic. The streets were beginning to look untidy, and not only because of the falling leaves. There seemed to be few sweepers around—maybe they lacked the brooms. Nor were there many police to be seen, simply a number of inefficient-looking young men in mufti with red and yellow police armlets. They had no visible function, but chatted with their friends at street corners.

On November 29th the Germans arrested more than a hundred members of the Fascist party at their headquarters in the Palazzo Braschi, at one end of our piazza. Many unexpected people and things were found on the premises, including a cow!

The retreat of the German forces seemed to be a heart-rendingly slow affair—just an occasional change of position—and the fighting in the south was harder than ever before, with the Allies making little progress. Although they attacked vigorously near Cassino and south of Pescara, the Germans resisted with do-or-die desperation, and progress northward averaged about half-a-mile a day. From time to time there were sounds of heavy bombardment, but always at some distance. We took little notice, and rarely discovered what had been bombed. At any particularly loud or near explosion someone always exclaimed facetiously, '*Lo sbarco!*' ('They've landed!'), but few people any longer believed in the likelihood of the 'landings', and some had given up hope that the Allies would ever reach Rome. That, of course, was the official German point of view.

The Germans had by now to some extent reorganized the supplies of food to Rome, and considering the enormous limitations and difficulties they did it rather well. Action against the excesses of the black marketeers had been made more rigorous. There was a shortage of salt and matches; the ration of the first was just over half a pound a month (half the normal consumption), and of matches one box a month. Smokers came off worst, and we sometimes saw one passer-by stop another, in the act of lighting a cigarette, and beg a light in order to save a match.

The children enjoyed Christmas, with the decorations (rather skimpy), a Christmas tree and a party at the house of some friends, and the journey home after dark in a *carrozza*. But afterwards, with news of the Allied armies making slow but steady progress and an increasing number of attacks on Germans in the city, new orders appeared on the walls. These orders appeared so frequently that people rarely stopped to read them, but on this occasion they were so all-embracing that they had to be taken seriously. Anyone giving hospitality to an irregularly inscribed person—i.e. one with false papers—was responsible for that person and could be punished by German (military) law, being liable to the death penalty. As the whole of Rome was more or less divided between the hiders and the hidden, the complications were innumerable. Nor was it permitted to change one's place of residence. It looked as if by March 1st, when our old ration cards expired and new ones would be issued, many people would be without even the small amount of nasty bread they could at present get hold of. At the end of December, however, when the census was carried out on which the issue of the new cards was to be based, something went wrong: either unintentionally or on purpose, there was much confusion at the booths, and some doubt as to whether the census would after all be possible. As for the order about changing addresses, many people continued to do so exactly as they had done before, risking the consequences. Nor did the porters at the apartment-houses collaborate with the police, as they were required to do.

Early in December some optimistic vendors had started putting up their stalls on the Piazza Navona in preparation for the Feast of the Epiphany, just as they had done for so many centuries. When I first went to Rome ten years earlier these little wooden shops had extended all the way round, giving the appearance of a piazza within a piazza, especially in the evening, when the shop flares made a circle of light. This year only four were put up, and three of them were taken down as soon as the small stock of figurines had been sold. The one remaining stall-holder was brave to carry on, for the weather was icy. One or two vendors appeared with hand-carts, selling wooden toys—all that was left of the joyous fair which delighted every child, and which had been the *festa della Befana* (though not always in the Piazza Navona) for heaven knows how many hundreds of years, developing on the evening of January 5th into a gay uproar which lasted until the early hours of the morning.

The Befana was an old pagan festival which, with the rise of Christianity, became the Feast of the Epiphany. The Befana herself was an old witch who was reputed to bring presents to good children and to castigate the naughty ones. I suspect that she is the origin of Mother Goose, for she too flew around on a broomstick—and only recently did these broomsticks disappear from the celebrations on the night of January 5th–6th.

The new year came in with cold, crisp weather and a bitter

The Piazza Navona from inside a booth at the Befana fair.

wind. Provisions became almost non-existent, without even the customary vegetables. Meat was unobtainable, and the poultry shops, which had generally supplied some kind of poultry at a price, were now so besieged by the crowds that it was almost impossible to squeeze into them, and totally impossible to get out without tearing one's clothes. Since our cook was the size of a small jockey, we were rarely lucky.

The streets were full of stange sights—people carrying heavy pieces of furniture, aged tricycles propelled by ragged youths, weird old lorries running on charcoal, which often broke down. One day I watched a small man shepherding two nice fat geese down our piazza; he whistled, and they followed at their leisure. However, when he wanted them to turn down a side-street they decided otherwise, and began a complicated toilet. The little man was patient, and for nearly fifteen minutes he waited before he tried to persuade his charges to continue on their way—but to no avail. Eventually he enlisted the help of two young men, one of whom caught one of the geese and tucked it, squawking loudly, under his arm. The other bird was so alarmed at losing its companion that it waddled anxiously at the heels of the owner, tripping over the irregular paving stones in its anxiety not to be left behind.

CHAPTER V

As THE DAYS went by the various police forces became more noticeable in Rome. There were seven organizations in all, usually working separately but at times together (except for the Nazi S.S., which everyone feared and abhorred), always jealous of each other. First there were the Italian metropolitan police, who, generally speaking, were in league with the city population, for it was they who warned the Jews on the eve of the Nazi pogrom against them, so that the great majority 'disappeared' and thus escaped deportation and death. In addition there were the Fascist police, aggressive but not so sure of themselves; the O.V.R.A., a sort of Fascist Gestapo who usually worked with the German S.S.; the Italian armed forces police—army, navy or air force—often the most helpful; the German S.S., the terror of everyone, from whose hands there was no escape; and lastly the bogus police, posing as representatives of the *questura*, but really intent on blackmail and robbery (a phenomenon which had apparently been rife in France for some time).

Therefore when a friend or relative or the friend of a friend was arrested or spirited away, it was first necessary to try to establish which police force was responsible. This ascertained, the next step was to locate the missing person. When he had been found, one or more of the other authorities who had not been involved in the arrest had to be induced by various means, ranging from inciting rivalry to plain bribery, to liberate the victim. These searches were difficult, and could also be dangerous, because they required contact—at least through an intermediary—with the Germans or with die-hard Fascists in authority, and also the goodwill of these people. Tact and patience were needed, and always when the would-be liberators were almost mad with anxiety and fear.

The main prisons were two: the Regina Coeli for the men, with a women's political section, and the Mantellate, which was the common prison for women, cold, dirty, and of dreadful gloom. Besides these there were the various villas or apartments of detention run by the S.S., where the basements were carefully arranged places of ingenious torture, while above were comfortable apartments for the officers. Occasionally some contingent of the German army could achieve a lightning rescue from one of the prisons, but not from the hands of the S.S.

It is difficult to convey the continual anxiety and tension prevailing in the majority of households, with disaster rather like a doodle-but, for ever circling overhead. It was not so much direct arrest for some particular subversive action which we feared, for life itself was just a chain of such activities, as the possibility of accidental implication in a round-up, involvement with the bogus police, or even mistaken identity. It was therefore desirable to remain as quiet as possible, and to be seen rarely; but as Enrico carried on with the bank, going off on his bicycle every morning, and as our house could never be for ourselves alone, this desirable state was seldom achieved.

Our large and rambling palazzo was built in the seventeenth century without regard to comfort or economy of labour, and was therefore impossible to run without inconvenience and fatigue. There are two small courtyards, tortuous corridors, small terraces, and an uneven tiled roof. The postal address of the back—or rather side—door bears no relation to that of our front door, and as we kept no porter or door-keeper and there was a bus stop within yards of our entrances, where there were always groups of people patiently waiting for the inadequate transport, it was not surprising that we were frequently visited by those seeking refuge. It was often impossible to send them away. So we had to make a rule that the visitors remained invisible to the outside world and never went out unless they left for good. However, we had our 'permanents', and one elderly Jewish gentleman came for one night and stayed for five months. Nevertheless we escaped detection, possibly because we were listed as friendly, or at least not hostile, to the Germans (we were not hostile to them as a nation), but we did take great precautions. Our inmates camped on the second floor, with the shutters almost closed and the beds never made up during the day. No spare clothes or other possessions might be left visible or easily to be found, and there was an alarm signal on which our 'guests' were expected to repair to the roof, shoes in hands. This, I think, occurred only once, and it was a false alarm because the Germans were looking for bicycles, and of course they never did other than strictly obey orders.

Our elderly household struggled along heroically. Mario, our wonderful little cook, suffered from a double rupture and was not supposed to carry heavy weights, while his wife, who was older than her husband, was almost blind. The faithful Pietro, who had been badly gassed in the 1914–1918 war, never gave in. Nor did the aged sister of the cook, toothless, incomprehensible but endearing, who dealt with the family laundry in the courtyard fountain and tried to placate my poor mother-in-law, who otherwise, except for our visits and trays of food, was quite alone with her manias. The huge brass double front door, which in normal times was open all day, remained shut, and the bell was defective, so when someone sought admittance they had first to be scrutinized from an upper window before a detour was made round the house, followed by a trip down the steep marble stairway to admit the visitor through the smaller side-door. Owing to the possibility of being denounced through careless talk, it was not possible to acquire new domestic help, so the children camped in the drawing-room, which was in fact also our living-room. By February we had to keep them away from school, as they had not yet reached the age of discretion. However, we had a trusted 'Signorina' who looked after them in the mornings, and for exercise they played in the Piazza Navona. Because of all this we tended to know little of events beyond our own small world.

None the less, news filtered through that the resuscitation of the Dictator by the Germans had been fruitless, and that his health continued to deteriorate. He was a tool in the hands of Hitler, and was quite unable to save his son-in-law Galeazzo Ciano from being shot, together with other Fascists, after the German-staged trials in Verona, in January 1944, of the so-called Fascist 'traitors'—i.e. those who had voted against Mussolini and the ending of the war at the last Grand Council the previous summer. Ciano had always been anti-German, but had not had the courage or the inclination to step down from his post as Foreign Minister at the outbreak of hostilities. With more foresight Count Dino Grandi, the leader of the revolt, had already fled the country, together with other dissidents.

The consternation at the death of Ciano and of the others was very great. The general feeling was one of despair that such a thing could happen. For Italians one of the most important things in life is to present a *bella figura* to the world—to cut a good figure; and to feel that Italy must be showing herself in such a bad light added to the general depression. I often heard people saying, 'We're no good', 'We're hopeless—we'd be better off under the English or the Americans', 'We don't know how to govern ourselves', '*Ci fa schifo*' ('It makes you sick'). Maybe the dollar had its attractions. Not even the young seemed to have any mind or any will. The Germans had got fed up with us some time ago, and I couldn't help feeling that they had reserved some vendetta for us which would shortly become apparent.

On January 13th we had a heavy bombardment on the outskirts of the town. It developed into a real air battle, and people ran out on to the piazza to watch, but when the bombing shook the windows they took shelter in doorways. We saw the bombers clearly in a bright sky. We were all getting weary, but realized that the worst was yet to come. The road to Cassino, so long contested, was giving way, and we began to hear of a new line, the 'Gustav line'. There would, we supposed, be another one after that—an endless demolition, piece by piece, of central Italy. There was another epidemic of 'time-' and hand-bombs, not large ones, but they wrecked German lorries and dumps, and one day there was an explosion in the forecourt of the Palazzo Borghese. A boy walked in and placed a parcel on the running board of a German lorry; soon afterwards it exploded, damaging some of the windows near the main entrance. There was an epidemic of arrests, too, mainly of Fascists, but also of people who had tried to be too clever. These were the result of wheels within wheels of the Fascist party, and were quite incomprehensible; but we could be arrested by so many different authorities that one rarely knew what to expect.

The heavy bombers were now operating from Italian bases, and the drone of their engines was almost a daily occurrence. '*Sono loro!*' ('There they are!'), people said, and when the planes were visible everyone got very excited and stood about in groups pointing them out and counting them. When, as often happened, the bombs fell (always on the perimeter of the city), the people showed next to no consternation. It seemed odd to me that they did not seem worried by the almost certain death of neighbours or even friends. Our children were quite gay and callous about bombing raids; for years they had heard of hundreds of victims, the dead and the wounded, so that it had become a normal everyday affair.

On January 20th we had a particularly heavy raid, with bombs falling so fast that it was a continuous thunder. Three days later the news came that the Allies had landed all along the coast south of Rome. But we heard nothing official—no announcement on Rome radio, or proclamation of a state of emergency. Not for two days did we learn that the Allied landings had been made without any effective opposition, the objective being to cut off supplies from the German defenders of the Cassino front. On the 26th, Rome radio announced that Velletri, about 30 miles south-east of Rome, had been occupied by the Allies, and that Cassino had at last fallen. We had no idea when the Allies would reach the city, and it was disturbing to think that if they delayed the Germans might decide to defend it; rumours were already flying round that people living on the outskirts had been asked to evacuate their houses, and that barricades were being built on the road leading south. By five o'clock the streets were deserted, though it was still broad daylight, and we could hear the continuous rumble of the German armoured cars passing along the Vittorio Emanuele Corso, though it was impossible to tell in which direction.

Contrary to our hopes, the invasion force made no spectacular advance. Both sides seemed to expect a big tank battle, but it was unclear who would be the attackers. In the meantime people in the city continued to be arrested. One lot of Italo-German hostages escaped, and no one knew who would be arrested instead. Generals and admirals implicated in the Badoglio surrender were still on trial, but it was difficult to know who was and who was not a 'traitor': it all depended on the angle from which the matter was viewed. The people continued a sort of passive resistance on the quiet.

Enrico profited by the lull in events to make a hurried visit, armed with the necessary German/Italian permits, to Cafaggiolo to settle various matters there and at Il Trebbio. He went by car, and we hoped the road would be fairly clear—though it seldom was those days—and that he would not have difficulty on the return trip. It was trickier coming south, and of course there was always a danger that the Germans might commandeer the car, if they were so ordered. Luckily he arrived back in a couple of days. Contrary to expectations he had had a comparatively easy trip, impeded only by heavy German reinforcements going south, from Tiger tanks to troops on foot. All was in good order at Trebbio, and everyone had been delighted to see him, and praying that the war would not reach them. The countryside was, they said, quiet now that the 'patriot' guerilla hands had left the district. He was able to bring back two hams and other things—marvellous!

He returned just in time, because the fall of Rome was imminent. The Germans had brought down reserves from everywhere possible, and were furiously attacking the bridgehead at Nettuno, south of Rome—it seemed at last with some success. The Allies had entered Cassino, but the remains of the fortress abbey were still holding out. It was all painfully slow, incredibly destructive and infinitely depressing. All the people who felt they were in danger spent their days rushing from place to place to hide, regardless of orders forbidding any change of address and making obligatory the declaration of everyone living in every house. It was pandemonium.

By the end of February we were still where we had been a month before (except that some six German divisions had been hurried from the south of France, northern Italy and Yugoslavia). The spearhead landings at Anzio and Nettuno had not altered. In the shops prices were rising steadily, and flour and farinaceous goods were not to be had for any price whatever. Politically we were rather worse off: the internal confusion remained, with the result that the Germans took whatever they wanted. The much-discussed 'open city' existed no more. We heard that Hitler had decided to defend Rome, and Churchill was prophesying another Stalingrad—just propaganda, perhaps, but terrifying for the citizens of this most unheroic city. All we could do was to hope that the issue might be terminated, or, better still, the war itself terminated, on some less populated battlefield, and soon, for by the spring the Romans would otherwise suffer terribly from lack of food and other necessities.

As best we could we continued our uneventful life, while the battle for Rome continued less than 30 miles to the south. When the weather was fine the advantage was to the Allies, who largely depended on their superiority in the air to weaken the enemy concentrations and to confuse them during the attack; when it was wet the Germans gained. The latter were about to launch a third attack to try to break down the bridgehead sufficiently to turn it into a rout into the sea. Their second attack must have been terrible in its concentrated ferocity of tank- and man-power crowded into a front of less than a quarter of a mile along a stretch of the road between Albano and Anzio, with wave after wave of attackers. After it was over the ground gained was described as a few square miles of blood-soaked no man's land. The German casualties were very heavy, and one friend saw many buses full of badly wounded go slowly by, with corpses heaped up on the top covered with tarpaulins.

There was something apocalyptic in this vast and concentrated holocaust of mechanical fury, this battle of battles for the city of cities—thousands arrayed in war against the 'anti-Christ'. Rumour said that about ten divisions were by now massed against the bridgehead at Anzio, in preparation for launching the third big attack. We heard that if General Kesselring failed to defeat the Allied forces in this sector he had decided to make a withdrawal south of Rome, but no one believed it.

Drastic measures were again being taken against young men of eighteen to twenty-five who failed to report for service, but very few of them responded to the call-up. As a result a system was introduced by which the police of each district had to supply a quota for the labour corps, and there were spasmodic round-ups and house searches. Fortunately we were not disturbed. We were also lucky to receive further consignments of provisions from Cafaggiolo, only one being lost in transit. We had even got used to not being sure of anything and of living in a state of uneventful uncertainty—always hoping for a more stable future, or at least for one that would be less nerve-racking. The only real comfort of the twenty-four hours was the moment of curling up with gratitude in a comfortable bed under one's own roof with a still sound hot water bottle, realizing the plight of the thousands of refugees (many of whom had lost everything they possessed) camping in the Tritone or the Gianiccolo Tunnels, or in caves and grottoes on the outskirts of Rome, with little covering and less food.

We were told that there were 700,000 refugees in greater Rome. Those hiding among the rafters of the churches were perhaps more fortunate than those cooped up in small apartments with greater danger of discovery. Some of them became rather daring, and a few officers even joined in social gatherings; but they never realized that their own danger—that of transportation to a German P.O.W. camp—was far less than that which could be meted out to their protectors. Happily, as few Germans understood Italian they were usually accompanied on their searches by Italian police, who very rarely pointed out to their colleagues that the men interrogated were not Italian. In fact, even the Germans had little heart for their job, and they soon gave up trying to round up these fugitives.

It was a complex pot-pourri of tragedy and farce. Few families were without heart-rending problems, and Virginia's piano teacher—the ample-bosomed, cheerful mother of a grown family, with a Russian husband—was no exception. She had no fats or oils of any sort in the house, and no prospect of getting any. Her husband had some illness and needed a special diet, and now his supplementary rations had been cancelled. Her son, an officer in the Italian army, was a prisoner of the Germans, and she feared he might be sent back to fight against the Allies. Apart from what she could earn, the family had no source of income. Nearly sixty, she spent her days hurrying from house to house to give music lessons and to accompany her daughter's dancing classes for small children, battling with buses which became steadily rarer, with shopping, food queues and cooking.

The stories of escape, evasion and recapture were innumerable, and often very entertaining. One concerned an Air Force pilot who was a bit of a dandy, and used to go round to tea and bridge gatherings in Rome (it would be difficult to suppress these in the

Eternal City) smartly dressed and wearing a black felt Foreign Office hat. It was naturally thought at the time that he was rather too audacious, and in fact one afternoon he noticed that he was being followed by two Fascists. Unable to shake them off he stopped in front of a shop window, and as they came up he turned as if to pass them. He was stopped and asked for his papers, but his false identity card could scarcely suffice, and he was asked to accompany his captors, which he did, walking between them like a lamb. He noticed that they carried their revolvers in the holsters, and felt that if he could make the corner of the street before they could fire he had a good chance of escape. Suddenly, he socked one on the jaw and the other in the stomach, and sprinted to the corner, which was only a few paces from his original destination, and disappeared unseen by his pursuers into a big doorway. Racing upstairs, he discarded his coat, borrowed a macintosh and another hat, and then sauntered out again past the Fascists, who were in a flurry of uncertainty on the threshold.

By the second week of March we had gone back to the daily air raid alarms of a few months earlier. The target seemed to be the railway yards, and there was much damage to private property. The situation was rapidly getting out of hand. After a heavy raid on March 7th some districts were without gas or water, and even some of the fountains had stopped flowing, though in many districts they were the main water supply. Some people had to go as far as a mile to get any at all. Until then we had been extremely fortunate, inasmuch as we had continued to enjoy nearly everything needful; but now we too were waterless. However, a watercock on the Piazza Navona was opened, and people clustered round it like flies on a carcass, with every kind of receptacle. It had turned cold again, too, and few people had any means of heating their houses.

One of the main targets near the station was the slaughterhouse and the canning factory where the Germans prepared food for their troops. This had been hit in the raid, which perhaps was just as well, because the misses had been causing appalling havoc and loss to the inhabitants of the tenement houses.

One day I heard a story of local interest, though I had no means of verifying it. During one of the round-ups the young men of Prati, who had been taken for labour service, were held in the barracks on the Via Giulio Cesare, and, probably as a punishment for attempted escape, or maybe because of a total lack of supplies, were kept without food for two days. Their cries of *'Pane, Pane!'* could be heard from the street. A crowd gathered, and relatives tried to bring food and clothing to the prisoners. When their help was refused by the Italian militia, who were on guard, the crowd turned nasty. A pregnant woman who had a son in the barracks refused to be put off, and insisted on trying to bring food to her boy. In the ensuing confusion she was shot dead by one of the guards. A free fight followed, and four of the guard's companions were killed by the infuriated crowd. This woman had the most amazing funeral, to which hundreds of people contributed. In the face of this kind of opposition the Germans suspended the round-ups, though by the middle of March they had collected only about five or six thousand of the fifteen thousand required.

After two days the water partially came back again—not the main supply but the *acqua vergine*, the Trevi water, which supplies much of the low-lying old Rome. It only came as far as our courtyard, but our chauffeur, who had become a great handyman, arranged a contrivance with pipes to raise the water by a bucket from a terrace above the courtyard. Mario the cook had already managed to supply water to the Aga cooker by means of pipes from the gutter on the roof, so when it rained we even had hot water!

The bombing continued, but the main station was not attacked. In our part of Rome, though our house sometimes shook and the windows rattled, the noise and blast were mild compared with what was experienced on higher ground. It seemed to us that the 'enemy' were using much heavier bombs than before. One day there was an attack on a purely residential district and several small houses collapsed, with the residents buried in the debris.

On March 12th the Pope spoke to a crowd in St Peter's Square. Everyone expected some great announcement, above all that the Germans were leaving. His Holiness was preceded by much ringing of bells, which seemed to suggest there would be news of importance. On the contrary, he merely expressed his sympathy with all the afflicted, but led us to expect further trials and losses, while at the same time condemning the destruction and its perpetrators.

The water shortage continued. For us it was mainly drainage that was affected, but other households had severe problems. People came to our courtyard from a mile away, and Enrico sometimes took a bottle of water with him when he was paying a visit. One day he returned with a turkey. Though he had had to pay an immensely inflated price, we were overjoyed to have it, for, though the new ration cards had in fact been issued, food was now truly scarce: flour, beans, potatoes and rice no longer existed.

With the advent of spring it was good to have the sun, but we were all weary, weary and disheartened; most of us were hungry, and many were ill. The previous September, Rome had believed that her plight would last for only a matter of weeks, and since then every month, or thereabouts, had seen a new offensive by the Allies—supposedly the final one. The terrific onslaught on Cassino still continued, in which it seemed certain that none of the Germans could survive; but they were still there underground, fighting heroically. The armies at Anzio had not moved, bogged down on the plain. Nothing had changed, except that we no longer believed that we could be 'rescued' soon, or that the Germans were leaving under threat of the Second Front, which in January had been declared to be imminent. Because of the bombing thousands of people left their homes early in the morning and returned in the late afternoon, spending the day in the Villa Borghese or some other park. Nevertheless the population remained patient and humble, and when they cursed, their target was not the American bomber crews; they were more likely to consider their trials a punishment from God, even though somewhat unevenly distributed. The Vatican, which had already done so much to help, had by now sixteen communal kitchens open for the poorest people, and it was hoped that they could arrange something similar for the *petit bourgeois* class, who suffered perhaps more than anyone, as they could not earn on the lucrative black market.

The situation was made worse by the refugee population fleeing from the battle-fronts south of Rome. Some arrived with nothing, not even their precious gold rings and little earrings, which the Germans had appropriated. Most of them had been herded into trucks and lorries, regardless of the distribution of families and friends, and despatched indiscriminately northwards, generally unfed, so that they should not impede the military operations. Pathetic and terrifying stories trickled through: one lot spent sixteen hours in crowded railway carriages at Rome station before being moved on, and were subsequently bombed by American planes, with many casualties. In another group a poor mother found herself with her four very small children on a lorry going north. It stopped at some wayside place near Rome, and she got off to try to find a little water for the children, but when she returned the lorry had gone, Her two babies were twins of four months, while the other two were too young to say their names. She had no relatives or friends in the lorry, it was impossible to get milk for the babies, and she had no idea where the lorry was bound for. However, we were told that hundreds of children got lost daily, so this was nothing very exceptional. How thankful we were to be in the centre of old Rome, so far undisturbed—indeed, the only Germans we had ever seen at close quarters were tourist soldiers on the Piazza Navona, and even these now seemed to have disappeared.

Our water supply was back to normal by this time, and we still had something to eat. But the strain of the autumn and winter had left its mark. Time had stolen not only our tranquillity, but a year for each month that we had lived through. Some people looked fifteen years older; meeting an acquaintance in the streets, one's immediate reaction was, 'Good heavens, have I aged so much too?' The civic authority of Rome did next to nothing to help the war victims—at least, we knew of nothing very effective. There was no central office for rehousing, and air raid casualties were left in the streets to fend for themselves. This was not from callousness so much as the difficulty of knowing who was responsible; there was no central authority, no one in control, and therefore little possibility of bringing any project to a successful conclusion. There was still no gas supply, and the electricity was low and uncertain. We heard that arrangements were afoot to give free passage to anyone who was willing to leave the city, presumably in the empty trucks which came in with food supplies.

We began to long for Il Trebbio, and wondered if and when we should return and what we should find there. We knew that if the next big line of defence was on the Apennines, Cafaggiolo—which is on the old main road, once the pack-road, between Florence and Bologna—would be involved in a general destruction. But in the unpredictable havoc of war often the unexpected happens, so we still lived in hope, and were fortunate in that, so far as our personal property was concerned, we had lost only two cars. We had begun the winter with our few valuable possessions hidden away as securely as possible, but gradually we had returned them to their original places, to be able to enjoy them for at least a little longer.

But in some ways our situation was getting worse. The bread ration was reduced to about 3 ounces a day, and only about 1 lb. of rice per head was distributed during March. Of our servants, only the cook's wife and sister were still on their feet, both over seventy. With other people's goods and furniture stacked all over the house, it looked like a cross between a warehouse and a tenement building.

Only some exceptional event roused us all from apathy, such as the quite awful affair of the Via Rasella at the end of March. At about five o'clock in the evening a German lorry full of soldiers was blown up—by a time-bomb placed in a dust-cart, I believe. Thirty-two German soldiers were killed outright and seven more died afterwards. The immediate round-up of all residents there brought terror and havoc, though most of these people were later released. By way of reprisal the Germans massacred 320 people, some from the street where the incident had taken place and the rest from the Regina Coeli prison, there for minor offences such as helping the 'patriot' bands, writing for clandestine newspapers, or merely suspects. These unfortunates were taken to the Ardeatine caves on the Appian Way and machine-gunned in batches. Then the sides of these old passages were blown up, burying the dead and those still alive.

I knew one poor old man, ill with cancer and haemorrhoids, who lived in the street. He was out for a stroll at the time of the attack, and was knocked down as he tried to return home. When he eventually reached his door he found the windows of his apartment broken, the doors wide open and not a single soul in all the house. I think he must almost have sunk down and died, for his old wife was his only living help, and without her he could not fend for himself. Mercifully she, with the rest of the occupants of their floor, returned home next morning.

In the middle of April alarms and air raids began again on the outskirts of the city, but we never knew where or what damage had been caused. Food supplies continued to be chimerical, but we had heard that there were food ships somewhere, which, it was hoped, would be able to bring their cargoes to the city. With our ration cards we were able to get a little salt, a few eggs, two tins of condensed milk and some matches, and on the open market we could buy vegetables. Luckily Rome is surrounded by market-gardens, whose owners, with the aid of hand-carts, rapidly made small fortunes and helped to keep the populace from starving. For the rest there was only the black market, which grew daily less hopeful. One day the cook miraculously found half a sheep, and was very pleased with himself. But nerves wore thinner and thinner. A couple of bakeries were rushed by the crowd, and in the medley that followed there were several casualties and, they said, some dead.

All our immediate world and his wife and family took to parading in the Piazza Navona on Sunday evenings. This new fashion was, I suppose, due to the impossibility of going further afield. It was remarkable how well-dressed the public could still be, with only a proportion of the children wearing wooden sandals. The girls went in for skipping competitions, though the boys, who on other days made a great uproar with their impromptu football matches and fantastic ball play, on Sundays walked with great decorum, imitating their elders, or sitting round the now silent fountains. It was all very peaceful, and the want and deprivation were all hidden away successfully on days of festa.

But the bell for the dead tolled nearly every morning in the church opposite, and every day we had news of arrests. People kept their children from school for fear of real or false 'denunciations', and young boys from the age of eleven were enrolled for militia work inspecting houses. We had no complaints, however, about the regular German army, which behaved with great correctness.

I was sometimes astonished at the way in which 'normal' life continued—the celebration, for instance, of Virginia's birthday and her first communion, a wonderful function beautifully arranged by the nuns of the Via Lucchesi, a cloistered order. The large chapel was decorated as if for a wedding, with white flowers, and many of the white-veiled nuns in the pews behind the grille or screen which divided the chapel in half. The *prie-dieu* at which Virginia knelt was draped in white muslin, decorated with tiny trails of ivy and other greenery, and her stool was similarly decorated. With her simple long white frock and diaphanous veil it was an enchanting picture.

A telegram from the Pope made the service all the more impressive, and afterwards, with relations and friends, the Mother Superior and the Monsignore who had conducted the service, we all sat down to a breakfast of coffee, milk and brioches. Virginia even had the host of presents usual on this occasion.

We were fortunate enough to have a carriage to take us to and from the church, a fine but antique coupé, shiny black and borrowed from some friends, drawn by a splendid chestnut horse. Virginia sat demurely on the edge of her seat, holding her white prayer-book in her white-cotton-gloved hands, but Lorenzo was interested in the impressive blue-buttoned upholstery and the silk blinds that could be pulled down slowly, jumping back with a rush when you jerked a little tassel on the end of a cord. The Corso, when we reached it from the Piazza Colonna, was empty, and we trotted sedately down this thoroughfare, to the accompaniment of the sound of distant guns at the Anzio beachhead, with not a single car, German or otherwise, in sight. Our imposing patrician turnout was modified by the appearance of the stalwart coachman, who wore an aged, stiff straw hat.

CHAPTER VI

AT THE END of April I went off to have an operation which I had been postponing for months. All went well, but I lost much of what little weight I had, and felt like a walking skeleton. This, however, was by now nothing unusual in Rome; most of our friends had had to take in their clothes, and hardly anyone still had a suit that fitted.

The clinic was on the Via Flaminia, on the way out of Rome, and it felt much closer to the war. Bombs and anti-aircraft guns could almost always be heard, and at night there were battles between men with revolvers or machine-guns.

Enrico had a daily struggle with the trams and the infrequent buses, as the clinic was some seven or eight km. from the Piazza Navona. Courage, as well as patience, was needed to undertake the interminable journey, and sometimes it was only possible to get a very precarious hold on the running-board of whatever public conveyance turned up. The few buses which were still running provided to some extent a useful service, but they were certainly also a danger to their passengers; and when they broke down they could not be repaired.

When I got back home I found that a communal kitchen for black-coated workers had at last been opened nearby. Before eating there it was necessary to get a permit from the Vatican committee, but for the few lucky ones it was a real boon to be sure of a midday meal. By this time the Romans refused to work for money, but would do anything for food, especially as it was now much more difficult to buy edibles on the black market, much of the supplies from this source having been sequestered and distributed among the people.

For some time after I returned home I was rather immobile, and friends would come to tell me tales of horror and woe, and the war news. The Allied advance was continuing: Terracina had been reached, the Anzio front had gone into action on May 23rd, and the Appian Way was already cut near Cisterna. This success was mainly due to the fact that the Allies had every possible weapon, offensive and defensive, whereas the Germans were reduced to next to nothing, with no air support at all.

From my window I could watch the children taking part in the life of the piazza. Enrico either walked or cycled to his office every day, and came back for a late lunch. It was the greatest good fortune to live in the centre of old Rome in those days, for the Germans had divided the city into an inner and an outer ring; no German was allowed inside the old city without a permit, and anyone found there without an adequate reason was sent to the front. The outer ring, so far as we could make out, had been arranged to facilitate transport circumnavigating the city proper; it all seemed to be very well organized.

The swifts, annual visitors of great charm, had already started nesting under the tiles of the roofs, and every morning and evening they circled round, hundreds of them, above the piazza in a clear blue sky, chasing their food, whirling and darting with that whistling chatter peculiar to swifts which fills the air with life and continuity. From the piazza below came the clatter of small wooden-shod feet and the loud tinkering of a man who mended copper pots. Often there was the distant firing of heavy guns, the occasional clop and rumble of a passing cab as it rolled over the small square paving stones, the cry of a vendor, the barking of a dog, the chime of the hour from the big baroque church of Sant' Agnese, and the toll of the bell for the dead. Since the children's dressmaker, incapacitated by work and worry, had vanished from our horizon, I occupied my time lengthening and enlarging what I could of Virginia's clothes. Mending-cotton had become extremely precious, and the thread from one hem had to be preserved for the next.

So far we had had reasonably good news from our property in Tuscany, and had been able to get more supplies than we had expected, though on one occasion the men in charge of the lorry told us that at a small village near Arezzo some *partigiani*, or partisans, had held them up at gun-point and robbed them of everything. It could have been a put-up job, but was probably true. The *partigiani* were often difficult to deal with, as they insisted on being given supplies and money, and stole if these were not available. Some of the bands had good leaders, and were more or less civil in their dealings with the local people, but others were little more than brigands. Since we were right on the main Bologna–Florence road, this was a terrible worry for our *fattore*. We hoped that providence would see him safely through, because he was cautious by nature, and mercifully talked very little.

A native of Cafaggiolo, in normal times employed on the railways, brought us news from home. He came to Rome on a lorry and left the same way, and was very entertaining about the ways and means of negotiating the road from Florence, which was a perilous business. There were, he said, two Allied patrol planes just north of Rome which watched the road day in, day out, machine-gunning every supply column or lorry which they saw moving on the road. There was a sporting technique for the lorry-drivers of when to make the next dash forward for a few kilometres, before jumping out and making a dive for the nearest ditch, trusting to providence that the lorry would not be damaged beyond repair. The road was in a terrible state; many bridges were down or damaged, and in places the drivers had to thread their way through bomb craters or damaged or burnt-out lorries. It was not surprising that Rome had next to no supplies. The Germans were using both the Vatican and the Red Cross markings for military uses, so everything got attacked, which was depressing.

On May 25th the Allied forces of the Anzio bridgehead joined up with the main army coming from the south from Terracina, and after this they were at last able to forge ahead, cutting through the Alban hills. The situation for the Germans was rapidly turning into a débâcle; for two days there was a constant rumble of distant bombing, and the roads round Rome were never quiet, day or night. But then the Germans sent down four divisions from the north, including the Hermann Göring division, which had been posted north of Civitavecchia. Fortunately, because the roads were bombed so heavily these reinforcements lost up to 50 per cent of their strength, and the Allies claimed that they had taken 15,000 prisoners since the offensive began on May 11th.

The battle continued to rage round Velletri and the guns boomed all day, but no one took any notice of them. It seemed that this time the Germans really were retiring, and that the retreat to the north had begun. Already the remnants of the Luftwaffe were leaving, and the sky was clear. The city waited anxiously for the worst—that is, the destruction of many public services, with some nasty surprises as well. For ourselves we thought the contrary: that nothing would happen, and that one morning we should wake up to find one army gone and another about to arrive. We felt there must have been some agreement between the Vatican and the German High Command, for in Rome alone there were many thousands of wounded German soldiers—some said twenty, some forty thousand—and it seemed likely that for the Germans there would be no long-term advantage in making havoc of the capital of world Christendom. They had prepared a long list of hostages, which included all the influential people of the city in every branch of activity, but this they had now abandoned; in any case, very few of these people would have been found at home!

And so it continued, with the vast majority just coping and hoping from day to day. With the prices as they were, it was difficult sometimes to understand how the 'bourgeoisie' could manage to feed themselves. Apparently they did so by letting out part of their house or flat whenever they could (and this was not difficult, due to the enormous demand for accommodation inside the city). Then, as prices rose, they sold such of their possessions as they could spare. First went the silver and clothes, next the jewellery, then their treasures, and after that, for those who could, their 'old age' savings and the dowry which they had put away for their growing daughter.

In our local black market at Tor-di-Nona along the river, whereas formerly one had to go into the squalid houses to buy, and it was necessary to know just which one sold what—meat, beans, or whatever—now such goods as remained were put on view in the streets, and the crowd and pandemonium, not to mention the prices, were terrific.

On the evening of June 4th two people rang us up to say that the Allies had arrived in the city and the Germans were leaving. We all felt restless; and though we were profoundly relieved, almost happy, we had the urge to go somewhere or do something useful, or talk to someone about something important, or just celebrate with anyone we happened to meet. But apart from the fact that we suddenly felt very tired (the fatigue resulting from a relaxation of tension), there was nowhere to go and nothing in the least useful to do, as the streets were still quite dangerous, with bullets and bombs going off and incidents between Fascists and anti-Fascists, Communists and the retreating Germans—all, however, on a small scale. There were many heavy explosions between nine and ten o'clock that memorable evening, which we took to be the bridges over the Tiber being blown up (this was quite wrong—in fact, they were left intact). We went to bed, as did our last wartime guest, Joey Nathan of the Bank of Italy, who had been released that morning from the Regina Coeli prison, but no one slept very well; it was all too noisy, and some youths on their way home cried *'Li abbiamo visti!'* ('We've seen them!'), much to the joy of everyone.

Next morning I was awakened by the noise of crowds on the piazza, and there they all were: khaki-coloured lorries, jeeps and motor-cycles, and lots of soldiers encamped below our windows, all American except for one lorry-load of Italians flying an Italian flag. All the other vehicles had the white star of the Allied armies.

The widower doctor next door came out with two wonderful flags, made clandestinely—the Stars and Stripes and the Union Jack. The neighbours were bitterly jealous and the children in despair. The doctor's son came to the rescue by presenting them with the two small sample flags from which the big ones had been made. These the children attached to two sticks, with great pride and joy, and to the envy of all the other children on the piazza.

We shook hands with an American soldier, joked with the crowd, and exchanged solemn felicitations in French with a distinguished, white-bearded Pole who had also just been freed from the Regina Coeli prison. The company there, it would seem, except for small crawling things, was of the best.

The Americans stayed in the Piazza for three days and then left. After the first exciting and noisy morning they confined themselves to the southern end near the Moro fountain, and had well-organized billets within their roomy lorries. They once drilled below our windows (a rather sloppy performance compared with that of European troops), but for the rest it was rather like Hampstead Heath on a bank holiday. The local inhabitants (most of them poor) pestered the soldiers for cigarettes, the children demanded sweets or chocolate, but all were joyously enthusiastic. The Americans took it in good part and didn't seem to mind the swarms of children. As for the girls, they had a glorious time.

After a couple of days all shadow of decorum vanished. A wine shop was broken into and liquor appropriated, though it was subsequently paid for. A number of soldiers became rapidly and blissfully drunk, staggering back to their lorries in twos, supporting each other, as no doubt, in the circumstances, four legs were better than two. The girls who had run after anything in khaki went on necking parties in the jeeps, and there was at least one fatal accident. The fraternization was complete, not only with the fair sex but with boys of all ages and also the *carabinieri*; everyone was smiling and pottering about as though they had nothing in the world to do. What a pity it could not all have remained on such a pleasant footing; it would have been better if they could have left then, while the memory of those first free, careless days was still fresh, before the difficulties, the jealousies and the misunderstandings began to manifest themselves, not to mention the realization that Italy was still an occupied country, and a vanquished one at that. Still, at least we could begin to enjoy a feeling of freedom—the freedom from fear.

The front line was now in the vicinity of Bracciano. The main roads were crowded with military vehicles of all kinds, and hundreds of tanks passed down the Corso Umberto at great speed, and along the Corso Emanuele towards the Via Aurelia, so that the Piazza Navona was at the centre of a warlike activity. Enrico was impressed by the armour and size of the American tanks, which looked much stronger than the German ones.

The day after the arrival of the Allied armies our telephone had been cut off, which was a great nuisance as there were no buses or transport of any sort. The only water came from the fountain in the courtyard, and there was no light and still no gas, which had been cut off some months before. Since it was June our meagre store of irreplaceable candles was holding out, but we missed the radio in those pre-transistor days packed with epoch-making happenings.

Troops of every nation and almost every colour were swarming about Rome, having a holiday after the trials of battle and the Anzio front. The Americans undoubtedly got along best, for they were out to enjoy themselves, and of course they succeeded. The British troops from all over the Empire had a uniform look of cleanliness and decorum which was much appreciated by the more discerning; they went about in pairs, and did not appear to mix very much. It was rare to see an English soldier and an American one together—partly, I think, because of the enormous discrepancy in pay. The Scottish regiments were very popular. Unable to get out and about very much, I had to rely on the reports of other people, but I was told that the following troops had all been seen in the city: Americans (the great majority, including coloured soldiers and Japanese Americans); English, Scottish and Welsh; New Zealand, South African, Indian, Colonial, French (Free French and De Gaullist, Moroccan, Senegalese and Indo-Chinese), Poles, Italians and Brazilians (who followed later).

We felt depressed about the future. Despite the pretence that a government had been formed under Ivanhoe Bonomi, after Badoglio's resignation, it was quite clear that the Allied Military Government were in fact the rulers, and it was just an illusion that the Italians were running their own country. The new government was to reside at Palermo (it was impossible to imagine any government office working efficiently from there), and officials in the self-governing provinces could not be changed without permission from the Allied Military Government. The Italian appointments had been made from among the *fuor-usciti*, the anti-Fascist refugees, and were otherwise unacceptable to the people, and quite understandably nothing worked. Not to mention that in all probability this hotch-potch of a ministry was unlikely to last more than a few months. There were Social Democrats, Socialists, Royalists, and Communists of various hues, and a Secretary of State often had an Under-Secretary with opposing political views, so it was difficult to conceive how any policy or programme could be agreed upon.

Still, it was early days, and we felt that it was important not to be too discouraged. There were some hopeful signs at least. For instance, at the first meeting of the financiers at the Bank of Italy the new instruction sheet for credits, payments and exchange bore in very large letters the heading 'Financial regulations for occupied territories'. At the next meeting, a few days later, the headings on the order sheet bore the more hopeful wording 'Liberated Italy'.

On the domestic front we felt, by the middle of June, that we had touched bottom. Apart from having no water, light, gas, telephone or post, there was literally nothing edible left to buy, other than a few vegetables now and then: no tinned meat, no coffee (so much longed for), no distribution of extra rations. The restaurants were closed and there were no buses. There was little else to buy, and what clothing remained in the shops was fetching fabulous prices.

Then the black market really got going again, so that most of what was available for the troops became procurable also for the populace—at a price. The Neapolitans and the Americans, with the help of the Canadians, were the leaders in these activities. For some days we lived on horse-meat. Then, gradually, the blessings of 'civilization' returned—water and light for part of every day, the telephone and the radio for four hours daily. What was hardest to bear was the decadence, if not squalor, in which we all lived.

In the middle of June the numerous military contingents still encamped in Rome were requested to leave by the Pope, because of the danger to the city from air attacks, so in this respect life became more normal. But the 'liberation hangover' from which the people had begun to suffer was spreading, and many were inclined to criticize. So far as I could make out, from the point of view of civil administration everything was being done that could be—except, of course, that the military were not really the best people for the job. It was too early to doubt the future, but there had been few signs of enlightenment shown by the 'liberation' Allied Military Government command.

From a military angle things were going well. The Allied forces were racing northwards and were already halfway to Florence. The Second Front was doing wonders, and we felt confident of its success, though the destruction must have been of the Cassino variety—a wasteland. It was remarkable that within ten days of the landing both Churchill and King George had visited the battle zone; we felt that the English Channel must be pretty safe before the High Command would take such a responsibility.

Rome was getting along not too badly under its new ruler, Colonel Poletti, an Italian-born American; and though friction was rife everywhere, it all worked rather better than had been expected. On July 4th the first train came through from Naples—just one month after the fall of Rome. This was a great achievement, as all the bridges were down on the inland route.

But we felt that the moral depravity of the Italian people would take a long time to repair, if indeed it could ever be. After years of corrupt rule by the Fascists—graft, embezzlement of public funds, nepotism, etc.—it had suddenly become, during the German occupation, a patriotic duty not only to hide as much food as possible and to destroy and sabotage war materials, but also to cheat, deceive and carry false papers. The Allied radio propaganda had self-righteously continued to advocate such behaviour. It was too much to expect that the less well educated section of the population could understand that what had been right and patriotic a couple of months ago had now become a criminal offence; their actions and their way of thinking could only have been changed through painful re-education, which was not forthcoming.

In Rome each faction in authority criticized the others. The so-called Italian Government remained impotent and almost invariably offended, while the stock of the royal house of Savoy was low. In April, King Vittorio Emanuele, in preparation for a referendum on the restoration of the monarchy, had agreed to withdraw from public and delegate power to his son, Prince Umberto, as soon as the Allied forces entered Rome, and in June he had carried out this undertaking. The Prince, however, who was referred to as the *Luogotenente*—the substitute for his father the ex-King—rarely appeared in public or seemed to take any part in political affairs. The purge of Fascists was in full swing. Colonel Poletti was dynamic and, where strictly administrative matters were concerned, very good; but sometimes, in his impetuosity, consulted badly or not at all, so that the wrong people got fired or put into vacated jobs, to the delight or fury of their political rivals.

The people, meanwhile, got what amusement they could out of life. On June 25th, the feast of St Peter and St Paul, there was an almost mediaeval scene on the Piazza Navona—an organized football match. The playing-field was the territory between the central Bernini fountain and the fountain at the northern end. For goal posts the players used bricks from the protective wall, now partly dismantled, which had been built round the fountain. There were about eighteen players, and the more efficient of the goalkeepers played with bare feet. The mass of onlookers were rather too keen to encroach on the 'field', while the stone seats were occupied by the usual motley crowd which frequents the piazza on holidays, including mothers with prams and children of all ages, who got somewhat perilously involved in the game. From time to time a cyclist would ride across the 'field' quite unconcerned. A few evenings later there was a second football match, and on another occasion singing to an accordion in the moonlight. It was a pity the singers weren't Neapolitan.

Every day the reports of the Allied progress on all fronts became more exciting: the Russians were at Vilna, the Canadians were breaking through at Caen, the Allied armies had reached Arezzo and Leghorn. The German losses, especially in Russia and Poland, were enormous. But in England the flying bombs were dropping over London at the rate of 100 to 150 a day....

We were beginning to have unexpected visits from relatives serving with the Allied forces. Most of the British had been away from home for three-and-a-half years or more, and were beginning to feel that it was too long, though all admitted that the campaign in Italy was far better than in most places (an impression which they were to keep in the years to come, with nostalgic memories of the lively, welcoming Italians and the beautiful countryside).

The great event at the end of August was Churchill's visit to Rome. He talked to Ministers and to Prince Umberto, and, though no one expected any dramatic change, everybody appeared to be truly glad that he had come. The war seemed to be racing to a climax on all fronts. Paris had been freed, Romania was out of the war and Bulgaria was on the brink of being so. We learned that when the French troops landed in France they fell down on the beaches and took up handfuls of sand, running it through their fingers and kissing the earth itself in their ecstasy at returning to their native land. Then, with the onset of autumn, the Allies settled down to a sixth winter of war. We ourselves had much reason to be thankful, for early in September we had heard that Il Trebbio and Cafaggiolo had not been defended, and that the Allies had been able to occupy them without fighting. It was marvellous to know that the *castello* was not a mass of rubble.

We were fortunate in that Trebbio was on the German so-called 'Gothic' line of defence, stretching right across Italy, while the tower was a perfect observation post. Luckily for us, after the withdrawal from Florence the Germans had neither the time nor the military resources left to defend the castle; the tower had been mined, but their final withdrawal was so precipitate that little damage was done.

However, during the last few weeks their headquarters for central Italy had actually been the big glassed-in loggia room off the courtyard. To avoid detection they had not allowed any sign of their occupation: the doors had to be left closed, no buckets, paper, bottles, boxes or anything similar might be left around, all jeeps and mechanized transport had to be hidden under the ilex trees on the piazza or elsewhere under cover, and drapes were even hung over the glass of the loggia. This foresight saved the *castello*, for one day an Allied reconnaissance plane flew over very low, carefully scrutinizing the entire terrain. Satisfied that the High Command was not at Trebbio they bombed Cafaggiolo instead, happily without any very serious results.

In October Enrico, who for the past few months had been working with the Allied Financial Commission, was asked to go to America on a one-man exploratory mission, with the aim of making useful contacts for future financial reconstruction on behalf of our chaotic country. He was away for two months, arriving back just before Christmas, via New York, Newfoundland, the Azores, Casablanca, Oran (by mistake, owing to the weather) and Naples. He was greatly pleased by the success of his mission, and impressed by everything he had seen in the States, by the helpfulness and friendliness of the people he had met, and by his personal welcome in a country where he had expected to find some diffidence vis-à-vis an erstwhile 'enemy'. By contrast, in England there seemed to be a rather strong anti-Italian feeling. But the journey by military plane both there and back had been desperately uncomfortable and tiring. The seats were metal ones with no backs, and the least bone-aching place to travel, he found, was on the floor.

His report on his mission was so favourably received that it was considered advisable that he should return to the States, and the request came from Washington that he should be appointed ambassador there. In some quarters in Rome this suggestion would have been received with approval; but as he had had no experience of public or political life there would also have been great opposition, since all the political parties, especially those on the left, had fish to fry, and candidates to boost. The idea was a great surprise to us, and on the whole we were relieved that it did not materialize. Eventually, on the recommendation of Count Sforza of the *Partito d'Azione*, Professor Tarchiani, a journalist, was accepted by the Americans as ambassador, but, tacitly, on the understanding that Enrico would go too, as a minister and as financial and economic adviser. When I met Tarchiani, shortly before he left, I found him a studious looking man, quiet and likeable. His wife, also a journalist, went with him. The plan was that the children and I would, perhaps, follow Enrico in the spring, though in fact we did not do so.

Enrico had a busy time before leaving for Washington, seeing, among others, Prime Minister Bonomi, Parenti (the Communist Minister of Finance), de Gasperi, leader of the Christian Democrats, and his old friend Introna, Governor of the Bank of Italy (who under the Fascist regime had been dismissed from his post when he had refused to accept an I.O.U. from Mussolini). He also saw Prince Umberto twice. Since the flight of the King the Prince had become very different from his former self: he read everything, and was interested in the political situation. Previously he had been kept too much in the shade, but with responsibility he had gained courage. He tended to consult only the rather aged statesmen, but he did his best and was liked by all for his genuine interest and modest ways. He once told a friend of ours that his wish when he was quite young was to be allowed on a rainy day to don a macintosh and go for a ride on a bus!

CHAPTER VII

THROUGHOUT THE EARLY part of 1945 the military still swarmed round the city, usually on leave. Social Rome snaffled a few of the higher ranking officers, but on the whole the soldiers just entertained one another at vast expense. The British Embassy people scarcely dared meet anyone in case they should be the wrong ones—that is, either of the Ciano world or one of the few ex-pro-Germans. There was not much evening entertainment because the streets could be dangerous at times: theft by assault or crime on a more serious scale caused the police many headaches.

To our joy, we were able to spend that summer of 1945 at Il Trebbio. I had, in fact, been able to get to the *castello* for a few days in March, having obtained permits from the Allied Military Command. The 190-mile journey in a somewhat rickety car was tiring, and I remember (how could I forget?) seeing so many derelict military vehicles, either ditched or destroyed along the route, especially on that tortuous climb up to Radicorfani where there was no cover whatever. (This stretch of road had become known as 'Ruddy-coffin' to the British soldiers in 1944 when they were pursuing the retreating German army.) There were countless temporary Bailey bridges, but I was surprised to notice so many others under repair or already reconstructed. Alas for the lovely Florentine bridges; only the Ponte Vecchio was left standing, and the approaches even to this were impassable owing to rubble and ruins. It was a sad sight to see only the piles of the other bridges standing up out of the river Arno.

Tired and hungry, we were held up at dusk and in the rain at the road divide just below Il Trebbio, for we were then on an 'American military road' and without the necessary permit to proceed. My explanation that I only wanted to go to our own property 'up there'—pointing to the tower just visible on the skyline—was of no use whatever. A non-commissioned officer tried to use the field telephone to Firenze, but time passed and nothing happened. The G.I.s joked and smoked in the dimly-lit tent (civilians to them were inevitably rather tiresome impedimenta), while everything seemed to drip in the darkness. *Pazienza!* Suddenly the field telephone worked, and I was told that we might complete our journey, but accompanied by two soldiers on motor-cycles to be sure of the veracity of my statements. So our car climbed the steep hill preceded by the outriders, arriving to a great flutter of excitement among our small community which was as gratifying as it was entertaining.

Little by little, with tears of emotion, all the tragi-comic panorama of events was recounted. The Sisters of Charity had been confined to part of the *castello* while the Germans (later the High Command) occupied the rest. We were told of the first truck-load of furniture, bedding, radio, etc., which had been removed by the Germans, and how two of the nuns had raced off next morning to complain of the despoliation of the orphanage, that is, of church property, demanding that it should be returned immediately. At midnight the *fattore*, who was by then living on the piazza at Trebbio, was woken by a banging on his door. Terrified by the prospect of arrest, he opened up to find that most of the furniture had come back, minus the bedding and the radio. The nuns had a permit for the use of a cow, so, whenever an animal was about to be commandeered, down rushed Suora Luisa—the most garrulous of that community—her white coif flapping in the breeze, to produce the permit, which referred, of course, expressly to that particular animal.

The head gamekeeper had had a narrow escape from being shot because of a list found on his person of the names of the members of our shooting syndicate. The Italian word *bandita* aroused the suspicion of the Germans—though it means roughly 'enclosure' or 'preserve'—as did the fact that the man had one German mark in his possession. He certainly looked like a bandit or a brigand but he was no partisan, though quite unable to defend himself. Anyway, for some reason the German officer had decided that he should be shot, and had loaded his revolver for this purpose, when the gamekeeper's heroic and very beautiful wife, Vittoria, rushed forward and knocked the pistol out of his hand, letting forth such a flood of furious explanation in the lovely Tuscan language that the German officer was incapable of further action. Eventually an interpreter was found and the misunderstanding rectified.

They had all had difficulties with the 'patriot' bands, which in our part of Italy were mainly ex-soldiers and others who had turned themselves into fairly benevolent brigands for a living. The Germans eventually rounded them up, but not before they had burnt out two of our hill-farms as part of the job.

During the last weeks, when the German H.Q. was at Trebbio and before the general retreat northwards, they had advised the nuns to allow themselves to be evacuated with the orphans to Bologna for their own safety. The nuns resisted strongly, praying to be left to their own devices: so, instead, they encamped in the chapel on the Trebbio piazza, which they turned into a dormitory. All the menfolk who were left had for a long time, off and on, been hiding in the woods by day and in the empty wine vats and elsewhere by night, and only the old people and the children were left to carry on as best they could. During the last days of conflict the chapel had provided shelter not only for the orphans but also for the *fattore*, who took the opportunity of sleeping under old Suor' Giuseppina's bed for safety in the tiny confessional, while the gardener squeezed into the hollow altar.

Eventually the Germans left, only twelve hours before the arrival of the Americans early one morning after some desultory shelling (I think it was on August 9th). They came along the old pack road, which for so many hundreds of years had been the main road for the merchant caravans and other travellers. They had a tremendous welcome, and all was noise and bustle. After the first surprise and awe the children swarmed about the jeeps and the tall gangling American G.I.s, while the nuns fluttered rather helplessly around. The men reappeared from the woods and the vats while the odd chicken was noisily chased for the pot, everyone laughing and happy, and the soldiers did not seem to mind being mobbed—indeed, they must have been used by then to such confusion. Trebbio tower became a useful observation post, and later, when the Americans were comfortably installed, General

Mark Clark, their commander, climbed the steep stairs to view the rearguard of the German lines on the Apennines.

During the difficult times after we had left Trebbio for Rome our local girls had hidden many things, and on our return we found little missing, considering the circumstances. Our *fattore* was a man large of frame and with a fine head, but of few words; he rejoiced in the name of Pompilio—though the children called him 'Pimpo'—and he more than anyone had reason to rejoice at the arrival of the Americans, because he had successfully disguised the vast threshing machine as a large wood-pile, carefully supplying the occupying troops with all the wood they needed. He had lied like a trooper when asked to produce the machine, which would have enabled the Germans to appropriate the precious wheat, for the thresher was, of course, registered with the *comune*, or local administrative office in the village, and if someone had given him away he would in all probability have been shot.

We had been fortunate in losing comparatively little, and most of the cattle had been hidden in the woods above us, but nevertheless there was much to repair and replace, and strangely enough we found pieces of furniture which did not belong to us and some of ours in other people's houses. Trebbio was indeed lucky to have escaped tragedy of any kind. Other districts had not always been so fortunate, though sometimes the stories were comic rather than sad. There was, for instance, the tale of a neighbouring *massai*, or farmer's wife, who at the approach of the military had hurriedly hidden a couple of her menfolk—they were always liable to be conscripted—in a tiny loft directly above the bread oven. On the arrival of the Germans they commandeered a pig and asked her to roast it in the oven. In terror that her family were about to be cooked alive she managed somehow to make the Germans understand that her oven was out of order, and diverted them to a neighbour's farmstead.

The intermittent return of our peasant soldiers, climbing our steep hill unannounced, always very tired and with their knapsacks on their backs, was cheering. They usually had rather grim tales to tell, and you could see that they had suffered. Great was the rejoicing in their rural homes. Little by little all seemed to be returning to normal, except for many supplies which were still difficult to obtain.

We had expected that autumn of 1945 to be quiet on our hilltop. Instead, a number of people appeared without warning and stayed or not as they felt inclined. Among them was Enrico's nephew, who, taken prisoner at the beginning of hostilities in Yugoslavia, returned from northern Germany. After his release he was attached to some Allied Occupation group as an English interpreter. As he knew next to nothing of that language, and as among his colleagues were a Frenchman, a Russian and a Pole, none of whom knew any language except his own, the resulting confusion resembled that of the Tower of Babel.

One day the British Admiral Sir Guy Warren, with his Flag Lieutenant, staged an impromptu football match on our croquet lawn to amuse the children. We also had a visit from Antonio Berti, who, like Giotto of the Renaissance, had been born on a farm in the neighbourhood, and while tending his sheep on the hills above the *castello* had often tried to model the Trebbio tower in the mud around him. He had become a well-known sculptor in the classical style, and he was happy to be able to pay a social visit to the restored Trebbio, the romantic ruin of his childhood.

Enrico left for his third visit to the States while we returned by car to Rome. This time the journey was far less eventful, but we did stop for the night at *I Tatti*, Bernhard Berenson's lovely villa. He was glad to be back there after the difficult war years in hiding. Although rumour had said that he was in the Vatican, actually he had never left Florence.

It had been wonderful to spend those weeks in peace in the country and find so little damage, when at times, cut off in Rome, we had pictured everything reduced to ruins. While we had been away de Gasperi had become Prime Minister, and the Americans were preparing to go home. The children were back at school, rehearsing for a Christmas play, and life was not difficult, though Enrico was held up at Casablanca on his way home, much to his despair, and unable to get back for Christmas. So began uneventfully the year of 1946. The weather that winter was cold at times, and sunny, but there was far too little rain for the coming summer's crops, and Enrico came back from a visit to Cafaggiolo very depressed about the general outlook, political and agricultural.

The spread of Communism in Italy, especially in the central

regions, is often mystifying to foreigners.* So is the fact that the Italians themselves seem to consider their brand of Communism different from the Russian variety, and can see no danger in it for their country. So far as our part of Tuscany was concerned, the young of today, and the generation which preceded them, were in a sense brought up on this doctrine. It started even before the war ended, when the Russian troops worked their way up the Adriatic coast in the wake of the retreating Germans. They distributed largesse freely to anyone who had helped, or claimed to have helped, escaped prisoners after the Armistice, whereas the other Allied partners required an elaborate screening of applicants before any monetary payment or even a certificate of thanks could be issued. This practice unfortunately soured the majority, who had so willingly assisted the fugitives without thought of reward, though they would have been proud to have had a memento to hang on their walls.

Soon after the cessation of hostilities some of our brightest peasant lads were lured away to the north for a course of political indoctrination, their parents being compensated for their absence from the farms. On their return they were all agog to impart their newly acquired 'knowledge', and there were organized clandestine meetings after dark (for such activities were illegal), which of course we were unable to prevent. Eventually a small red pennant appeared above our threshing machine, and when this was discouraged by the authorities it was replaced the following year by Picasso's dove. But our farm people were never disrespectful, and there was little or no animosity; often, when one of the younger generation appeared in the agent's office at Cafaggiolo with some carefully hatched request, and received the invariable answer '*Portaci papa*' ('Bring your father along'), as likely as not he did not come to support his son's application.

Political enthusiasm was soon on the wane, for the Tuscan peasant, like all his now nearly extinct race, is a cautious individual and avoids getting too involved in anything. But the indoctrination had taken root, and for many Communism has become *il Partito Nostro*, Our Party.

* Not long ago I read, on how reliable an authority I do not know, that there are more Party ticket holders in Italy than there are in the Soviet Union.

In March I went to London for a few weeks. The train journey was not difficult, but slow for the first part, since most of the bridges in Italy were still being rebuilt, and this often involved a detour on a temporary wooden structure. Almost all the track still consisted of single lines, necessitating long waits for passing trains. It took nine hours to get from Rome to Florence, and eleven from Florence to Milan.

My first impressions of London were not of general destruction, and I was glad to see many places and institutions as I remembered them. But as I saw more of the city, from a bus or on foot, I realized the extent of the damage: empty spaces here and there where houses had once been, whole districts which had ceased to be, and rows of windowless and abandoned dwellings. I also met the queue complex. This at first amused and then maddened me. Not to stand in a queue was considered anti-social and anti-democratic—in fact, it was almost a moral obligation. The habit seemed to have got under people's skin, and one saw people fall into a queue when there was no reason to do so. Everywhere there seemed to be great crowds on the move the whole time, and I found it all rather bewildering.

On the way home I spent a night in Paris with Gladwyn, who was much occupied with the setting up of U.N.O. He had taken part in its first sitting in London, and was certainly one of its godfathers. When it assembled at Lake Success in America he had had a fan-mail, I was told, equal to that of Hopalong Cassidy (wasn't he a star cowboy?) in appreciation of his great 'St George' act in defeating the dragon of the Russian representative Malik. I admire my brother, a dedicated European, for his great integrity, his loyalty towards his colleagues, his generosity towards his political opponents and his immense capacity for work.

That summer we lived through the referendum for the monarchy. After the rather ineffectual King Vittorio Emanuele had with difficulty been persuaded to sign the deed of abdication, barely three weeks were left for the royalist campaign. At this time the stock of the royal House of Savoy was at a very low ebb, but, once the still rather retiring Prince Umberto had been declared King Designate, supporters sprang up like mushrooms all over the country and the campaign got speedily under way. The Prince was received with much enthusiasm wherever he went. He was dark, tall and charming, and he toured the country tirelessly, but the time was too short for him to be able to reach the many rather remote districts in the south where the proletariat had been skilfully fed on republican doctrines; and, though the whole of the southern half of Italy was at heart royalist, many people voted in what they felt was the safest way—in fact, as they were expected to do.

At first it seemed as though the royalist cause was winning, but as the votes came in from the south they amounted to a total of only 64 per cent, which was not quite enough to offset the staunch republican north. By June 10th we were supposed to be celebrating the advent of the Republic, but in Rome there was a real lack of any enthusiasm and no flags; instead a feeling of depression settled on the city, and a distinct feeling of loss. The final vote was in favour of a republic by a narrow majority (51-49 per cent), but the validity of these figures was hedged about by doubt, for there had been many illicit practices ably administered. Nuns had been told outside the polling booths, where they nervously repaired for the first time, to put their cross on the emblem they did not want, and in the south some of the mesmerized and uncomprehending voters had been told that, as the King had run away, they could vote for the Queen instead! Others thought they were voting for a RE-Pubblico—a new form of monarchy, for 'Re' means king in Italian. One poor woman, found crying outside the Quirinal Palace, explained that though she had voted republican she had had no idea that the royal family would have to leave the country.

The behaviour of Prince Umberto was beyond reproach during those difficult days of indecision and frustration. He tried to be helpful: he received all those who wished to see him and remained calm when others were losing their self-control. It had fallen to Senator Bergamini, with the aid of Enrico, to raise funds for the monarchical cause, and Prince Umberto, with the consent of his wife Marie José of Belgium, had offered their own family jewels to help the campaign. None the less deceit and malpractice triumphed, and so, seeing no other solution, Prince Umberto left Italy without any formal abdication because, in fact, the referendum did not represent the will of the majority of his people.

Before he left, Enrico had the pleasure of handing him back his jewels—intact, as was the wish of his supporters. The Prince's eyes were moist as he said goodbye. Not only was Italy, we knew, losing a man who could have been a good head of state and constitutional monarch, but the people were certainly losing a real friend.

That summer at Trebbio was the tenth we had spent there (we had missed only 1944), and it might have seemed that we were returning to the rural life of before the war. But times were changing fast. The growing tendency to mechanization, the easy transport, the radio (aided by political propaganda) caused the disintegration of the *mezzadria* system, and the old-fashioned way of life inevitably began to vanish. Social customs changed and the standard of life became higher. Unfortunately fate decreed that the change was too precipitate. The less well educated sections of the people were bewildered by the sudden accessibility of so much they had never had before; it engendered unrest, and the peasants themselves really did not know what they wanted—certainly not to own the land they worked, for they rightly suspected that they might find themselves worse off.

I remember their first acquisitions after the war, when the fashion was to buy suites of modern shiny veneer furniture for the *novelli sposi*—to furnish the room for the arrival of a bride into the family. These prized novelties were hauled up our hill on straw-lined farm-carts drawn by the white *vacche*, so that all the world could see the shine of the polished plywood and the brass handles of cupboards or chests (apt to fall off after some time in use). Then motor-cycles became an indispensable acquisition, and later there was a race to keep up with any neighbour who had been bold enough to buy a motor car and had learnt how to drive. The refrigerator followed where there was any electric current, and then bathrooms became a sort of status symbol. Factories sprang up near Florence and Prato, and the big motorway across the Apennines needed many labourers. Thus the *mezzadria* pacts which decreed that a peasant had to have a permit to work elsewhere were ignored, though they were still legally in force, and by the mid-fifties there was a definite flight from the land. The emancipated girls wanted nylon stockings, high heels and even long gloves, and naturally did not fancy working on the land as their mothers had done. Nor did they wish to marry young peasant-farmers. So the over-worked farmer's wife had less help for her cheese-making (from sheep's milk), for the care of the domestic animals and poultry and for furnishing provisions for her family. Nevertheless the agricultural life continued as it had done in ages gone by, with the rotation of the crops, though the bulk produce tended to diminish and the families were smaller.

A Tuscan Peasant.

Before the war Enrico had begun to tap lost springs and take the water to the farmhouses, and his plan for the irrigation of the Cafaggiolo plain had helped him to gain the trust of the ever-suspicious *capoccia*. He continued the work now, and went on restoring the farmhouses and bringing electricity to those near the main supply, but the joy had gone out of the work and, alas, disillusionment soon followed; the families who had been rehoused in better conditions usually quarrelled, and instead of feeling gratitude or pleasure for the improvements, they were for ever thinking up what next they could achieve. None the less, they remained outwardly pleasant and civilized in their ways.

There were still church festivals, and I remember well the autumn procession, a sort of harvest thanksgiving which has now disappeared, a manifestation of the last century. This procession boasted a beautiful white *baldachino*, a scalloped canopy, carried on six poles, under which walked the priest, carrying a reliquary. He was preceded by two men bearing painted lanterns of Renaissance design, and at the head of the procession was a large white ensign with a red cross; on windy days it took two strong men to keep it aloft. The young men carried all this paraphernalia, the older men followed, and lastly came the women, draped in black, and the children, all chanting 'Ave Marias' and prayerful supplications for the salvation of their souls, their *anime*, in the nasal chant of rural religious practice in Italy.

The charming and ancient little church of Spugnole, perched on a spur of the hillside roughly parallel to our own, is now abandoned and silent. I think nostalgically of the three lovely bells which always rang the Angelus at midday; they were cast with silver and were of beautiful workmanship. In the early days after our arrival the poor old priest had to walk the two km. from this little church to Trebbio and back to say Mass, and sometimes I fear he must have felt it to be beyond the powers of his ageing frame, for I learnt afterwards that he used to hesitate along the route, hoping that one of the peasants might give him a raw egg or a glass of wine as a restorative, but in their cupidity they seldom did so. Now, of course, the priest arrives by car, but from the opposite direction, from San Giovanni on the old pack road.

When we first came to Trebbio there were hawks of various kinds to be seen hovering over the fields looking for their prey, and once I saw a golden oriole, but never, alas, again. There were hoopoes with their triple hoo-hoo-hoo call, those lovely crested long-beaked birds almost pink in hue, the black and white feathers on their wings catching the eye during their delightful undulating flight. But these last years I have seen them no more. The hawks, too, have vanished from our land, and like the butterflies, once so numerous, may have left us for ever. The house martins have also been far fewer these last summers. They added much to the charm of this place, circling round the tower in pursuit of their food.

Were the game and the wild life very different in the days of the Medici? Besides the hares, partridges and pigeons, I suppose there might have been a few wild boar, and also deer of some kind to provide venison for the table. The hunting would have been with whippet dogs and hawks—indeed, hawking was a great mediaeval art, and the ger falcon, rare and lovely white bird, was the prerogative of the great. At Trebbio there were a couple of painted iron cages for hawks on the front terrace, and Lorenzo il Magnifico, the grandson of old Cosimo, was an expert at this sport; but no doubt the poor peasant resented all the damage to his crops, and woe betide anyone caught poaching.

Donatello, the sculptor, had been given a *podere* on the property by his patron Cosimo, but there is no record of its location. However, as he was often absent, the wily *capoccia* cheated him so successfully that he complained bitterly that he never saw half the produce, for the peasant was for ever hatching up ingenious reasons for his failure. Donatello lost his temper, and exchanged his farm for a pension.

The flight from the land covered about a decade. When the outlying farms fell vacant the Forestry Commission encouraged the planting of trees, but this work was subsequently hampered by the lack of foresters or of sufficient hands to supervise the young plantations. The Christian Democrat government did make constructive efforts to counteract subversion by starting local clubs for the workers, but the wind of change was blowing far too strongly and these clubs could not take root. Pimpo expressed it rather well; he said, 'It's a government of priests, so what can you expect?' Let us hope that some day, with patience and with courage, our successors will be able to render unto Caesar only the things which are Caesar's—that State and Church can administer separately, complementing each other, and that man can eventually become 'wholly' civilized.

CHAPTER VIII

EACH WINTER IN Rome life continued to return to the seemingly normal, though inevitably change is always working without halt; it is really only a question of the pace. In some decades it seems as though the times are stationary, with custom and habit apparently permanent, but in other decades—as in our own—it races, to the confusion and bewilderment of nations.

The yearly festival on our Piazza Navona of the Befana, the Feast of the Epiphany, became each year more commercialized, the booths more sophisticated, the electric and neon lights more brilliant and variegated, with the *ciociari*—the peasants of the Roman Campagna—dressed by now in a parody of the clothes of their native Abruzzi, with bright green ribbon wound round their black felt hats and around their white, much-too-clean leggings. They marched like automata up and down the piazza, sounding their age-old lament on pipe and bagpipe, but, paid by the *comune* to 'put on a show', they asked no alms, as had once been their custom. The several Father Christmases—the *Babbo Natale*—trying to persuade the parents to buy toys for the Red Cross, usually only succeeded in frightening the children instead of entertaining them.

At carnival time I saw a procession embodying an idea which I did not realize still existed in the minds of the Romans. A group of children were carrying a black-covered wooden box up the hill of Capo-le-Case, above Piazza di Spagna, bearing a notice, '*E morto il Carnevale*', purporting to be the funeral of the carnival. This, of course, must be an age-old custom common in other times, but

A street in Rome

Rome: Piazza Navona

Piazza Navona:
detail of the Bernini fountain

Villa Medici from the Pincio at the top of the Spanish Steps

The roofs of Rome—hiding places for many refugees

Piazza Navona from the roof tops

The figures of Castor and Pollux from the Capitol, and the Gesù church in the distance

Rome: roofscape

with the congestion of modern traffic it has become a most inappropriate activity.

None the less, the custom of parading the children in fancy dress in the streets during carnival time still continues, and that year there was a daily spate of participants caparisoned as sheiks, cossacks, cowboys, Chinese, *pompadours*, and so on. The more affluent among the proud parents exhibited their offspring from the vantage point of a *carrozza*, that old-fashioned four-wheeled cab of which there are an ever-dwindling number in Rome, the child or children perched on the open hood. But even these popular customs will before long be discontinued in the crowded scramble of city life.

Before the war there was one day in the year when the populace placed gifts, mainly of food and drink, below the little platforms in the streets where the metropolitan police stood to direct the traffic, these offerings to be divided out among their families. Though this practice continued for some years after the war it, too, became commercialized—so much so that the gifts were usually packed in large bags bearing the name of some firm in prominent letters by way of advertisement.

1950 was the *Anno Santo*, or Holy Year, when the big doorway to the right of the colonnade of St Peter's was opened for the influx of pilgrims from all over the world. By Easter there was a daily average of 25,000 visitors to the city. They arrived by air, by train, by bus or by car, on bicycles or even roller-skates, and usually stayed for three days. The groups toured the city under the guidance of some priest or lay leader, and on the Piazza Navona they invariably stationed themselves near the famous Bernini fountain of the Four Rivers, with its circular basin and obelisk of red granite. The elongated shape of the piazza is due to the fact that it stands on the site of the Roman circus of the Emperor Domitian, constructed on the arches of the stadium, which was used for chariot races. The pilgrims, unlike the crowds which once frequented the races, were very docile, and meekly followed their leaders, who usually carried placards high above their heads to facilitate their progress in the milling crowds of St Peter's Square, where frequently more than 100,000 people were gathered. Huge buses of all colours—red, green, yellow and blue—parked early below our windows on the morning of the feast of the Assumption of the Virgin, whence their occupants went on foot to St Peter's to be addressed by the Holy Father Pope Pius XII.

The grand finale of Holy Year was the beatification of the young girl Goretti, who, some thirty years earlier, had been killed while trying to resist rape. This ceremony was carefully arranged, for not only were the parents of the child present, but the assassin—now an old man—was brought forth from his refuge in some religious house, where, presumably, he had lived an exemplary life. All this appealed greatly to the thousands of the Faithful who were fortunate enough to have passes for the ceremony. What girl today would be beatified for trying to keep her virtue?

We were glad to see the *gamberi rossi* (literally 'red prawns') back again in circulation—the German theological students dressed in their bright red soutanes. This vivid colour was decreed in times past because the young men at the German seminaries were so badly behaved that the authorities wanted to devise some means of distinguishing them from other nationalities, so that they could be kept more easily under surveillance.

That year there were receptions at all the legations and embassies to the Holy See for the very many visiting cardinals. The gathering at the Spanish Embassy in the Piazza di Spagna was, as always, the most sumptuous, and the interior décor there of marble, red-damask-covered walls and heavy gilded furniture made a magnificent background. Up the grand red-carpeted marble staircase swept the crimson and scarlet robed prelates of the Church, accompanied by two or more prelates in black or purple, past the liveried flunkies holding huge lighted candles in gloved hands on each side of the entrance, and under the glare of arc lights—because some of these entries were being filmed. On they swept with the rustle of their taffeta cloaks along the marble flooring across the big entrance hall and through other rooms. They then greeted their host and hostess, whose genuflections were deep and genuinely pious, and proceeded on across the big dining-hall, where the buffet occupied the whole of one of the side walls, and into the last room, where circular dinner tables were beautifully arranged for these important guests. Some of the Roman aristocracy, known till recently as the 'Black' social world (those who had adhered to the Vatican and the Pope after the

Papal States had been confiscated at the unification of Italy in the last century), as well as others considered with special favour by the Church, were invited to join the cardinals at their banquet of lobster, champagne and other delicacies. The rest of the many guests jostled at the long buffet, with fare not much less varied than that served in the sanctum beyond. Here there were churchmen of all categories, but no nuns or women of any religious order. The majority of the throng ate this delicious and abundant spread with gusto, while others, the more humble, seemed a little lost and confused by all the grandeur.

The British Legation reception was remarkable by contrast. The entire area in which it was held was probably smaller than the entrance hall of the Spanish Embassy, and about six hundred invitations had been issued. The British Minister and his wife bravely tried to make everyone feel welcome, but the cardinals (happily fewer in number) were expected to stay in the small entrance room while the rest battled past them to the cocktails and sandwiches.

I well remember a dinner, beautifully arranged by the Dutch Minister to the Holy See and his elegant wife, for a powerful member of the Catholic hierarchy, large of frame and with a commanding gaze from light blue eyes. We had received an invitation for *grand-soir*, which meant white tie for the men but never full décolletée for the ladies, who knew they should arrange their toilettes with sleeves or drapes to hide excessive nudity. However, the day before the party we received a telephone message to say that the *grand-soir* was off and that we should arrive less grandly caparisoned. We knew that this change had been necessitated by the death of one of the Cardinal's colleagues, though the funeral was yet to come. So the guests all arrived sober of aspect and demeanour, mostly in black, though two of the ladies were in white and the Cardinal was in day-attire of black with red trimmings. At the end of the excellent meal the principal guest silently raised his glass of champagne towards his charming hostess; was he toasting, I wondered, a safe passage for his erstwhile colleague?

Holy Year coincided with our first introduction to what were known as 'flying saucers', and at the time I wrote in my journal, 'This is the year of flying discs reported to have been seen in the most diverse places in Italy. These visitors are supposed to come either from Mars or, failing that, from some secret arms experimental station in the U.S.S.R.' True or not, Virginia was convinced that she saw a cigar-shaped space-ship high up above Rome, moving sideways in a clear blue sky.

Social Rome returned without difficulty to pre-war ways, but with more circumspection. People were careful to avoid ostentation because of the political climate and the fear of the 'tax-man', who was often snooping around to gauge the financial resources of the citizens. The dinners and receptions continued, but the Roman nobility were seen less at the embassies and in diplomatic circles, the number of which had increased enormously. The cost of entertaining rose sharply, and it was difficult for any ambassador to arrange a well-balanced gathering, or very rarely a select dinner-party.

When Enrico had dined out before the first world war there had been only nine embassies, of which the Austrian and the British were the most *en vue*. In the 1950s they had increased to nearly ninety, and the number was still growing. Some of these new representatives were housed in the old Roman *palazzi*, the one-time homes of the great families, where the rooms of the grand *piano-nobile* (first floor), sometimes with beautifully frescoed walls and highly decorated ceilings, were magnificent settings for entertaining, though the service departments left much to be desired: it was a mystery to me how those meals, so excellent, were produced so well.

Much of the private entertaining was financed with American dollars, but there was one exceptional Italian hostess, the excellence of whose parties was perhaps partly accounted for by the fact that she was really one of the last grand Edwardians, having spent much of her youth with her English relatives in England. Vittoria Colonna Caetani, Duchessa di Sermoneta, was an outstanding person, tall, dark, handsome and a superb hostess, though admittedly some people did find her a little intimidating. She wrote two books of memoirs and never tired of showing guests her beautiful apartment, with its many priceless *objets d'art*. She was also a good business-woman, and staged sales at her home of beautifully embroidered bed-linen and other useful household things of original design and good workmanship, some of which she had embroidered herself, and which her many friends and would-be acquaintances were most happy to acquire. One Christmas day, I remember, she jokingly remarked that really she did seem to live in exalted circles, having received game from the royal reserve near Rome, greetings from the Duce, and something or other—I forget exactly what—from His Holiness Pope Pius XII.

Vittoria had a lady's maid called Gertie, and she too was grand (she was sometimes known as the Vice-Duchess). She was the daughter of her employer's wet nurse, and was therefore what is known in Italy as Vittoria's *sorella di latte*, a sort of sisterly association. Her husband was the butler, and his sister was the cook, so the household was a family affair, which for the Duchess was very convenient. Indeed, her own convenience directed all her activities, though she could be generous to destitute friends, and, as she herself said when asked to subscribe to charity, 'I support the undeserving poor'. Gertie was a great standby; she knew her mistress's habits and needs inside out, so that, for instance, when there was some guest who she decided was either a bore or over-staying his or her welcome, she would discreetly intervene. 'Excuse me, your Grace, but the masseuse is here. Shall I tell her that you are engaged?' At this the guest made haste to depart, but Vittoria, the perfect hostess, was immediately reassuring; there was no hurry, the masseuse could wait for a few minutes. Yes, indeed, she was grand.

There always seemed to be some ex-royalties in Rome, among them the family of the last King of Spain, Alfonso XIII, which had come to live there before I married. The King lived at the Excelsior Hotel, while the Queen, Vittoria Eugenia (granddaughter of Queen Victoria), was at the Grand Hotel with her two daughters, the Infantas Beatrix and Cristina. They were still considered by the many royalists as very royal, and were much liked in Rome.

Enrico looked after the family's day-to-day finances, and both King Alfonso and Queen Ena used to visit him at the bank in the Piazza di Spagna—but separately, and usually to complain about the other. The Queen was large, handsome and fair-haired: she much enjoyed her bad bridge, and occasionally went out to the golf course at the Acqua Santa for a little exercise. One day I was detailed to play golf with her. Arriving in good time, I found her in a rather agitated state, because she had just met the King, who had told her that he wished to play with us. Quickly I volunteered that perhaps she would no longer need me—but no, we were all to play together. Now, threesomes on any golf course are not popular, but this one, composed as it was of three very bad players, was an event I shall never forget.

In those days the club was rather small and select, and most members knew each other at least by sight; so when our trio launched itself on to the course those behind us, realizing who was playing ahead of them, refrained from shouting 'fore' and going through, while those in front, recognizing who was following, waved us on and then stood by the fairway spellbound as our unexpected trio passed, because it was the first, and I think the only, time that the royal pair had been seen together in public in Italy. Thus their Majesties and my wretched self hacked our way along, getting into most of the ditches which abounded on the first nine holes of the Acqua Santa course, the Queen whispering to me that on no account were we to dispute the King's declared score. The frustrated queue behind us lengthened and the course before us was empty, though, mercifully, at the ninth hole the royal game was ended.

As far back as 1934 that golf club was still a small haven of peace in the country, where you could lunch on spaghetti and frittata (a sort of omelette), often in the sunshine of the clubhouse terrace, an old *casale* painted a deep red-ochre. From there one could see women in the shallow valley below dressed in long, full, dark skirts, filling their copper pots with the good water of the Acqua Santa spring and then carrying them away on their heads. Enrico always had an appointment with the skylarks on the first Sunday in February, an annual tryst which gave him great pleasure. It was not until the late fifties that they were finally driven away by the air traffic, the encroachment of the city, and not least the trigger-happy gunmen for whom little birds hold no charm. I think that apart from the disillusionment engendered by the agricultural revolution in Tuscany it was the loss of the lark song which Enrico felt most nostalgically.

These changes came fast one upon the other, and I remember seeing for the last time an ox-drawn cart on the course harvesting hay amid the noise of the motor-mower, the throb of two helicopters looking like huge insects in the sky, and the roar of a couple of planes circling overhead while awaiting permission to land at Ciampino, then the air-field of Rome. There was an old man employed by the club called Napoleone—no one knew how long he had been there: he preferred working alone, building and repairing culverts and walls on the course. One day I asked him his age, and finding that he was in his late sixties I wished him another twenty years of activity (any thought of retirement was quite alien to his nature). Well pleased, he answered '*Speriamo*', 'Let us hope so'.

The high-wheeled painted wine-carts had long been a daily sight ambling their way to and from the city and the Alban hills along the Appian way, with the two upright poles inserted in the rear of the cart holding the little wine barrels stacked in place. The driver's seat, large and well padded—for he often slept there—was covered with a collapsible sort of canopy which protected him from sun or rain, and these hoods were usually painted in good rural art and in various colours. The carts went right into the city, but each year their passage became more difficult and they were in greater contrast with the ever-increasing traffic, but even in 1960 I saw one slowly passing our house on the main thoroughfare. Usually these wine-cart drivers kept a little dog for company and to guard the cart, but this day the man was alone, and I instinctively felt that I should never see this scene again. So, too, with a couple of rural honeymooners whom I noticed outside the Quirinal Palace looking dazed but happy, she wearing a rather makeshift version of a one-time regional dress with long, dark, pleated skirt, a white flowered blouse under a lace-up sleeveless velvet bodice, and a head-scarf. But this was just a throw-back to other times—the brides today, even country ones, are very much more sophisticated.

For myself, after the war I had taken up my drawing and painting again, which had occupied me off and on since I was a child, when I had had a wonderful teacher, Miss Edith Cheesman. I was again fortunate, for I was given the possibility by a friend, Madame Jacques Ibert, the wife of the director of the French Academy, of working with her in the large private studio in the grounds of the Villa Medici. She herself was a good sculptress, and later we had an exhibition together on the Via Veneto. I felt as though I had inadvertently gained a Prix de Rome. Later Enrico fitted out a studio in the attic of our house, and I embarked on drawings of old Rome and eventually larger panels in Japanese inks which proved very popular. At first I sold in aid of the Red Cross, but afterwards just for private people or causes in need—a luxury in which not everyone has the possibility of indulging. In 1956 I had an exhibition in London for the Italian Hospital in Queen's Square, an excellent institution which is open to all nationalities and is staffed by the Order of the Nursing Sisters of Verona.

When we were in London a few years previously we had taken the opportunity of going to court, my mother to present me—belatedly on my marriage—and I to present Virginia. Here again times had changed: when I had been presented in the twenties I wore three white ostrich feathers in my hair, a three-quarter-length evening dress and a short train, but with only four inches on the ground, with my mother in black and gold equally caparisoned. We had spent a couple of hours sitting in our car in a long queue stretching right down the Mall in St James's Park, while the crowd peered into the cars making remarks about the somewhat embarrassed-looking occupants in their uniforms or evening attire.

In 1952, at one of the very last courts, it was quite different. Afternoon wear of almost any style could be worn, or even a coat and skirt. When we were all three ready to start, our hired car failed to arrive, and so we popped into a taxi and parked ourselves outside the large closed gates of the palace courtyard, where we met some old friends, also presenting a daughter. Eventually the big iron and gilt gates swung open and we all walked in, alongside the slow-moving cars which had been at the head of the queue.

In the large white hallway with the low flight of red-carpeted steps Virginia was heralded in one direction with all the other young for a pep talk by some palace official, while everyone else was ushered into the throne room, which is also the ballroom, but was arranged for that day like a concert hall with the royal seats on the dais. We seated ourselves in the second row and waited. The débutantes passed from left to right, making their curtseys first to the Queen and then to Prince Philip. They were pushed through at a good rate. The curtseys varied considerably from an awkward little bend of the knees to an old-fashioned *plongeon* to be practised at home before hazarded in public.

In Italy we had acquired a new President, but there were repeated elections and a plethora of political parties, sometimes as many as sixteen. In the 1948 elections the 'D.C.' (Christian Democrats) polled 52 per cent and the Socialists, allied with the Communists, 32 per cent. The figures for the latter remained fairly constant until quite recently, but the Christian Democratic majority tends to diminish a little the whole time, for we usually have either a governmental reshuffle or an election every year. A great deal of money goes into these political activities, and on one occasion, a municipal election, the walls of Rome were so plastered with posters and paper of all kinds that there was no room left, and the remaining propaganda was pasted on the pavements. The political scene became more and more confused, and has remained so, leading to many compromises, an art at which the Italians are past masters.

It was not long before Enrico closed his bank in the Propaganda Fide palazzo in the Piazza di Spagna. The occasion was the one hundred and eighth anniversary of its foundation by his grandfather. But, by way of compensation, he accompanied the other twenty-eight Italian delegates to The Hague conference of the European Federal Movement—the first of its kind. There were eight hundred participants, all guests of the Dutch Government, and the conference was held in an atmosphere of cordiality and hope—how soon, alas, to be dispelled, for there developed many different federal movements, to the Right or the Left, and many different concepts of how to proceed, with various nations expecting a leading role.

The old order ever changes, and about this time quite a few of the old Roman nobility left the scene. Within days of each other two Roman princes died—Ruffo Ruffo della Scaletta and Urbano del Drago. As in life, their funerals were somewhat of a contrast. Ruffo Ruffo died at his villa situated just above the Piazza del Popolo on the boundaries of the Villa Borghese gardens, and the funeral was at his nearby parish church of Santa Maria del Popolo. I had gone there that day for the anniversary Mass of the death of a friend, which was held in one of the transept chapels near the high altar. There were not very many of us, but all through the Mass the sacristans were feverishly getting everything ready for the funeral service which was to follow, and one of them more or less stepped over us in order to extricate a very dusty *prie-dieu* from another little chapel. At this point the bell rang for the elevation of the Host, and down on his knees the sacristan went, clutching his *prie-dieu* for support.

Shortly afterwards a group of the ancient Order of the Misericordia arrived, sixteen of them, all dressed in some sort of sackcloth, including pointed hoods with slits for eyes. These figures are now more often to be seen in pictures and old prints than in real life. They prostrated themselves at full length in pairs before the high altar, and then, bearing aloft a plain wooden cross surmounted by a rusty iron crown of thorns, filed out of the church to fetch the deceased. They returned with the coffin, also draped in sackcloth, and placed it on the floor below the altar steps, while the hooded escort, holding long lighted candles, flanked the bier. Also guarding the coffin were half-a-dozen soldiers from Ruffo Ruffo's old regiment: he loved his men, and had been president of a committee dedicated to the thankless search for the survivors of the Italian Expeditionary Force which had been sent to the Russian front in 1941, with such disastrous results, for by 1943 half its members had been killed or taken prisoner. At intervals there were bugle calls and the church was full of sincere mourners, people from all walks of life. It was a very moving occasion.

The other funeral was at the vast church of Santa Maria degli Angeli, which was built into the remains of the great public baths of the Emperor Diocletian. The form of a huge cross is more or less accidental, but at least two of the great vaulted ceilings are of the original construction. The main altar, as is not unusual, was draped in heavy black and gold, and the raised coffin was covered in the same manner. Underneath was spread a large carpet, coloured and patterned. The only flowers were a big cushion of white lilac and another of violets on the coffin, both very beautiful. On each side four footmen in the del Drago livery held massive candles in white gloved hands; to these were attached small placards bearing the family crest—a golden dragon on a blue ground. The livery consists of dark blue knee-breeches and frock-coats, with white, silver and cerise braiding and silver buttons, and white stockings. Beyond this imposing bodyguard were four more *camerieri* in black breeches and stockings with darkish blue frock-coats, and then the *maggiordomo* himself, in immaculate black. He had arranged many parties for his employer, and was arranging this function equally well, escorting relatives and the more important mourners to their allotted places in the black-draped choirstalls on each side of the coffin.

A few of the Roman families still use these lovely liveries on important occasions, but with each year that passes the possibility lessens. Many families, too, are dying out: quite a few have no direct heir, or indeed any heir at all.

Aid to Europe was by now well under way with the Marshall Plan, which was actually the foundation stone for a United Europe, and in 1949 Enrico had the good fortune to attend the Westminster Conference in London, where he read a paper on bimetallism. Conferences always seem to achieve less than is hoped, but at this one the initial agreement was signed for the Council of Europe, which in turn produced the European Parliament at Strasbourg.

Enrico used to enjoy his rare visits to London. Once he went further afield to Cambridge, where Lorenzo was at the university. Feeling that the occasion warranted lunch at the best restaurant, our son duly booked a table. But Enrico rather let down the side by politely handing back the delectable menu unread to the *maître d'hôtel*, saying, 'Thank you, but I would prefer lamb chops and mouse-trap cheese.' He always maintained that one could eat very well in England, and the weather he always found excellent!

Later, in 1956, I was invited to join a delegation to Vienna for the Congress of the European-American Association; the small Italian group was led by Ambassador Tarchiani. The Congress aimed at setting down their findings on the principles of Western civilization, but it was badly based from the start, because there was no guideline as to the geographical limits of Western civilization. Perhaps it should have been limited to Europe and North America. I looked up the Ten Commandments, as bearing on the subject to be studied, and found that perhaps only three can be said to be accepted as true guidelines in life today. During the conference sessions I noticed that nowhere was the word 'spiritual' mentioned. let alone Christianity, which seemed to be altogether debarred. However, one hopeful principle developed out of the Conference—that of 'Habeas Animam', to be added to the age-old concept of 'Habeas Corpus'; this of course acknowledged, even if indirectly, the existence of the soul.

We were entertained with grand meals in palaces and beer-halls, and I learnt how very few Congress delegates have any real wish or will to achieve even a tiny step forward on the path of the integration of ideas, or to establish international friendship, thus contributing something personal, however small. Instead, as soon as there promised to be a rather boring speaker, off most of them went to sightsee. The chairman, Prince Bernhard of the Netherlands, was absent, and the most interesting figure was Princess Kira, the Russian-born wife of the eldest grandson of Kaiser Wilhelm. She was good and charming, but seemed a little frustrated in the atmosphere of this would-be modern congress. There was, however, one charming rolypoly German woman, a teacher, I think, active and friendly, and I feel she must have been very disappointed with the outcome. Each delegation was supposed, on their return home, to review the findings of the Congress and draw up their conclusions in comprehensive form to send to America. Tarchiani did his best, but I later understood that our small group was one of the few which even attempted to do so.

None the less, even with such poor collective efforts the cause of a United Europe goes haltingly forward, and for the ultimate good of civilization we must continue to persevere.

CHAPTER IX

IT WAS NOT long after the end of the war that tourists began to infiltrate and often disrupt our splendid isolation at Il Trebbio. One Frenchwoman, arriving alone in a large car, upbraided us for the bad condition of the road; it was a disgrace, she said. Another day, when I was sitting in the garden, there appeared in our big doorway a rather flamboyant figure, also French, who told me that he had been looking for me everywhere to explain that he and his Italian colleague would be no bother, and would take all the photos he needed for his paper without disturbing me at all!

The big Florentine event of 1949 was the five hundredth anniversary of the birth of Lorenzo il Magnifico, when the city *comune* arranged a luncheon at Il Trebbio in April. Long trestle tables for more than forty people were placed down the fifteenth-century pergola. The well-known historian of the Medici family, Professor Gaetano Pieracini, was in a sense the real guest of honour, though there were a number of political V.I.P.s, including Giovanni Gronchi, who later became President of the Republic. Pieracini was charming but already a very old man. He was carefully shepherded by a niece, and I fear he must have found the luncheon rather a trial, for the day was unexpectedly hot, and the slatted bamboo screens laid over the pergola, though they afforded some shade, did not make it cooler.

As is usual on these occasions, the meal was too long, rendered more so by the various guests who intended to make speeches. So when Gronchi had spoken and there was a pause, I rose, thinking that my action would be the signal for adjournment. But no, the guests all clapped and made ready to listen to another discourse. Bravely I suggested that as it was really rather hot it might be better to repair to the courtyard loggia for coffee. This was greeted with hilarity and applause, and considered *molto inglese*, very English and practical.

Once indoors we manœuvred Pieracini towards a comfortable armchair, first showing him some sixteenth century painted Medici pottery, known in England as faience. He was very deaf, so I shouted loudly, 'Professore—Cafaggiolo', pointing to the pots, for there had been a small but famous factory of this ware, started by Pierfrancesco de Medici, which had produced pottery till the end of the sixteenth century. Seeing them he stretched out his arms, making a few halting steps towards them. '*Ma no! Ma no!*', he said almost incredulously, and touched them gently as though he had just found a long-lost treasure.

The next year we had military manœuvres in the Mugello, the origins of which dated from the end of the last century after the unification of Italy. At that time King Vittorio Emanuele I came to San Piero a Sieve to preside over these new military beginnings, accompanied by the British Ambassador, Lord Cadogan. The population was apprehensive of what these military exercises might lead to, for the destruction caused by Napoleon's troops was still a vague memory. They were haunted, too, by the more distant horrors of the destruction brought about by the warring states before the unification of Italy, and of the havoc wrought among the population in past centuries. Of course these fears were groundless, and all proceeded pleasurably for the majority, while the guns boomed out from the vast Medicean sixteenth-century *fortezza* above the village, reputed to have been in part designed by Leonardo da Vinci.

So it was that in 1950 we had a request from the military to allow them to use the *castello* of Trebbio as a base for operations. They also asked if they might place chairs on our *campo del cricket*, or cricket field, as they mistakenly called our croquet lawn, which they wanted to use for a lecture, *al fresco*, on military tactics. This of course we had to refuse. Nevertheless it was all a success, and the High Command left us with a flourish of impressive signatures in our visitors' book; there were nine generals, one admiral, and the excellent lieutenant who had done all the organizing, and whose signature ending the list was more modest.

We do not know much about the social activities of the people who lived at the time of the Renaissance, but at Il Trebbio there were hunting parties composed mainly of the family and their close friends. At other times there were smaller gatherings of the erudite entourage of the Medicis, men interested in philosophy, science, mathematics and literature, who met to discuss the latest theories or manuscript acquisitions from Greece or elsewhere. Although Il Trebbio had been built primarily for a summer home when the great heat rendered even Cafaggiolo uncomfortable, it was probably in the autumn, for the *caccia*, or hunting, that the *castello* was at its gayest. It is easy to picture the bustle and the noise at dawn, the falconer, the hunt servants, the leashed dogs, mainly of the whippet variety but also a local breed of retrievers called *bracchi* (white and liver coloured), and perhaps a horse or pony with saddle-bags, all congregated in the courtyard or near the large arched entrance awaiting the pleasure of their *signori padroni* to start off for the chase. Or on some other day they might return in the evening down from the hills with the rays of the setting sun behind them, illuminating the Trebbio tower and the walls with a soft pink hue, so beautiful with the back-drop at dusk enveloping the plain below in a blue haze. There would be flares in the courtyard while the game was being stored in the cellars and kitchen, the happy hunters recounting the excitements of the chase, and perhaps expressing anxiety about the fate of one of the falcons missing in a flight over the ridge of a hill.

Though the family usually lived in Florence, there was one lady, Maria Salviati de Medici, who made Il Trebbio her home for about fifteen years. It must have been extremely cold there in winter. The grand-daughter of Lorenzo il Magnifico, she was the wife of Giovanni the condottiero, who was her third cousin and was himself descended from the cadet branch of the Medicis.

Giovanni, her husband, had been left an orphan when he was only a few years old—his mother had been the famous militant ruler of the estates of Imola and Forti, the Contessa Sforza Riario. He inherited from her his fiery spirit and his courage. Even as a child he was wayward, rebellious and cruel, and he refused any instruction. When he was eleven he escaped from his guardian's house in Florence and walked the fifteen miles to Il Trebbio, which was his property. Here, with an older cousin from Cafaggiolo, he embarked on a life of dissipation. The *fattore*, one Viani, was a faithful henchman of the Medici family, and though at first delighted to see his small *padrone* he soon became disillusioned, for the boy was exacting and uncontrollable. Viani had to admit defeat and wrote despairing, and later desperate, letters to Giovanni's guardian, Jacopo Salviati in Florence (Maria's father), explaining that he could no longer cope with Giovanni, and that he was also rather frightened, for the boy was violent and brooked no restraint. Viani wrote in an uneducated and halting Italian, but most poignantly, that if he had to continue thus he would go mad! Indeed, it was not long before this youth had several homicides to account for, though because he was a third cousin of (the reigning) Pope Clement VII he was never called upon to pay the legitimate penalty for his barbarous actions.

At the age of seventeen he married Maria Salviati. She was devoted to him, but he led the life of a spendthrift till he was put in command of a company of Florentine light cavalry, and sent off to fight a local war at Urbino. He was a born commander, tall, dark and sharp of feature, with piercing black eyes; he was absolutely fearless, but though he could on rare occasions be generous he was habitually vindictive and sadistic, often paying his men with the sack of a city while he himself led a dissolute life.

In the meantime Maria, a gentle and perhaps rather anxious woman, lived with their only child Cosimo at Trebbio, trying to satisfy her husband's frequent requests for arms, horses, dogs and other things, while she wrote him frequent letters explaining that they lacked everything, even wheat for the bread and hay for the horses. She never got any answers—indeed, Giovanni did not know how to write.

The debts accrued, and her only consolation was her gentle, good-looking little boy, reserved and quite unlike his father, who participated in such amusements as the country could give him. He was jealously guarded by his mother, for the Medici had many enemies in Florence, so that Maria's life was a perpetual hazard. I can picture her so well, this harassed young mother in her long, full dress, her soft white coif falling on to her shoulders and her household keys dangling from her belted waist, looking wistfully out of the southern casement window, listening in the vain hope that her violent husband would send her some help or message, listening for the sound of horn or signal of approaching visitors with news. The faithful Viani did what he could, and no doubt was a great help to her, but there was no money for repairs, not even for the necessities of life. Once at least Giovanni did come home, but as always he was inconsiderate and demanding, for he sacked the good Viani with the words, 'He who eats my bread must obey me'. No doubt he had told the old man to do something that his conscience forbade him to do.

Giovanni delle Bande Nere.

However, this madcap commander died of wounds after a battle at the early age of twenty-eight. There is a tradition that he himself held the candle by the light of which his leg was amputated. He left this world unrepentant, believing that he had been a virtuous and honourable commander. He was known as *Giovanni delle Bande Nere*, or John of the Black Bands, and was one of the first soldiers to organize disciplined, uniformed troops.

Maria continued to live at Il Trebbio, during a period of much political unrest. In 1529 Florence fell to the Papal and French troops, after a truly epic defence by the Florentines, during which old Michelangelo himself helped to defend the walls. For three hundred and fifty years the city lost its freedom. However, Maria's son Cosimo was accepted at the court of the new ruler, Duke Alessandro de Medici, the natural son of Pope Clement VII; and when the Duke was murdered (by a cousin of the Cafaggiolo branch of the family) Cosimo, then aged seventeen, was elected as

Maria Salviati.

the new head of state, and many years afterwards became the first Grand Duke of Tuscany.

Poor Maria's cares and tribulations were at an end, and she left Trebbio to live in Florence; but she had suffered so much that her health was no longer good and she could not adapt herself to her altered life or enjoy the ease which she merited.

By a lucky chance, in the State Archives in Florence there exist inventories of the property and goods of the Medici family going back to the fifteenth century, which include long and detailed lists of the furnishings of Il Trebbio and Cafaggiolo.* Most of these inventories date from around 1500, but there is one for Il Trebbio from 1476. These inventories give a minute description of the contents of the *castello* and of their value. The chapel was very richly endowed, not only with the Botticelli *Madonna* but also with other pictures, velvet chasubles, altar cloths, golden chalices and other precious articles, though some of the most valuable objects were apparently kept in a chest in the room of 'Madonna Lixe'—probably the wife of one of the Medicis. The many other rooms of Trebbio also contained rich hangings and pictures, and the compiler listed even such humble articles as knives and forks, which were kept in the rooms of their owners, showing the value that was then attached to them. There were bed-covers from Ireland, and silk and damask from the Levant.

Most of the really valuable Medici possessions were kept in the family's town palaces, but there were rare and lovely things in the country houses also, such as Baldovinetti's altar-piece, now in the Uffizi, which came from Cafaggiolo. It is amazing how much of Il Trebbio has survived through five centuries: an original ceiling which still retains its vivid colour and intricate pattern, and the stone wash-basin, set into the wall, which Cosimo de Medici used for his ablutions.

To return to modern times, less concerned with intrinsic beauty, it must have been about the year 1955 that we had our first *festa*, or fête, at Il Trebbio. It was held to raise funds for maintaining an ambulance which was to be supplied by the Red Cross. Delivery was delayed, and in the meantime it became a political issue, as is

* For the details which follow, I am indebted to John Shearman's fascinating article, 'The Collections of the Younger Branch of the Medici', in *The Burlington Magazine* (January 1975).

all too often the case in Italy, for the Communists were determined that their Party should have the kudos of supplying the village with such an up-to-date acquisition. With immense haste they acquired a second-hand vehicle which they proceeded to adapt as an ambulance, while the rivalry between the two factions mounted apace. The preparations for the fête, which in itself was a great novelty, continued. But who would come? Would it be boycotted? Then there was the unexpected difficulty of the invitations. Who should be asked and who left out? Actually everybody wanted an invitation even if they had no intention of coming to the fête. Since I did not know the inhabitants of San Piero well I gave many of the invitation cards to the doctor's family to send to whom they would, but for them it was an insoluble problem because their writing might be recognized and their participation would please some people and displease others. It was all fraught with uncertainty, but finally the invitations were sent out with printed lettering, and were posted in Florence.

Virginia and the doctor's daughter, with a few other pretty local girls, were dressed in gay but rather makeshift peasant rig of times past, and some local musicians were engaged, but everything was surrounded with difficulty and frustration, for in Italy you need permits for, and taxes are levied on, absolutely everything, including every tune played and each glass of wine consumed. Dancing requires a special permit, which was beyond our means, and 30 per cent of the takings of the gate were due in tax, even though it was for charity.

Eventually all was in order; curiosity triumphed over political bias, and up the people all came in spite of the *comune* subpoena-ing the local taxi. There was no fixed entrance fee and the voluntary offerings were not spectacular, but all went well and everyone especially appreciated being able to go over the house, including the walk round the ramparts and the top of the tower. Among the guests were two local tax-men snooping around to see that no infringement was afoot and also scrutinizing each other, the more important suspecting the lesser. However, when towards evening most of the crowds had gone home, the second man invited Virginia to *far' quattro salti in famiglia*, which means literally 'four skips in the family'—and so all ended well with a little illicit dancing.

Then came the *coda* or aftermath of the fête, with the advent of the rival, Communist ambulance (the official one had still not yet arrived), and our excellent *parroco*, or parish priest, who is still with us, had to bless the bogus ambulance while a photographer took pictures for the newspaper *Unità*. In the meantime I had gone off to see the tax-man, the one who had suggested the four skips in the family, to deal with the 30 per cent of the takings. The conversation, after polite preliminaries, went something like this:

'Well, it was a pity there were not more people and the gate was small.'

'Yes, and the weather was not very encouraging, was it? How many people would you say were there?'

'Really, I have no idea. How many would you say?'

'Perhaps two hundred? And they were not very generous, I fear.'

'I quite realize that. Shall we say . . . ?' etc.

Finally an amount was paid at which Higher Authority would not quibble.

The Red Cross ambulance duly arrived, resplendent, and was much admired, but of course the financial resources of the village were barely sufficient to support even one such luxury. So it proved that the bogus ambulance faded out, having served its purpose, after the *sindaco*, or mayor, had preferred to send his wife to hospital in the more comfortable one.

Other *festas* followed, with far fewer complications, and to one of them came Alfredino Aiazzi with his accordion, still blissfully recalling the impromptu dance on the main road at Cafaggiolo at the birth of Lorenzo fifteen years before.

The next big *festa* was in aid of the hearse—because this was the only cause for which the local inhabitants could agree to cooperate, and even so not without difficulty. This time we tried a mixture of social grades, another innovation; but as some of the neighbouring proprietors, owners of villas in the vicinity, felt that to collect for such a cause could bring bad luck we stated that it was in aid of 'local assistance'. They stilled their fears by bringing their contributions in closed envelopes for the good nuns of the nursery school in the village. The day was fine and there was a buffet in the garden, and then before closing time quite a little crowd of our peasants gathered outside the big gates peering in at the party.

Enrico, relieved and happy that all had gone so well, flung open the gates and in rushed our people, just as they were, in their working clothes. Our good Maresciallo, of the carabinieri police force, thought for a few moments that he had a mini-revolution on his hands, but what the peasants really wanted was to see if there were any ices left for the children: it was a joyous finale.

Some years later, in the sixties, I knew that I could not do so much organizing and coping, and so I rather rashly suggested that a popular fête in aid of the local needy families, with games and competitions, might be a good idea, and asked the doctor's wife if she would arrange it. The result was electrical, with bright red posters so large that few people had sufficient wall-space to accommodate them! The newspapers, Right and Left, announced the event, and even the radio advertised the day. There were to be children dancing on the lawn, and I pictured them all waving red flags and singing the 'Internazionale'. Nothing of the kind. It was well organized, loudspeakers blared, and a large field was put at the disposal of the four hundred and more cars. The congestion on our hill was rather frantic, but there were no accidents. The house was almost stormed by holiday makers, with bottle-necks up and down the tower stairways, but, incredibly, there was no damage of any kind, nothing was missing, and not even the flower beds were trampled. Unfortunately the *popolo* were not generous, and some tried to enter without any contribution or else dropped the minimum into the large glass jar at the entrance. There were sack races and a tug-of-war, etc., and then came the question as to who should give the prizes. I declined with some suitable excuse, and in the nick of time appeared a well-known Florentine Christian Democrat Senator who willingly stepped into the breach. So all, yet again, finished well. The next morning the lady organizer found me, aided by the children of our tractor-driver, collecting orange peel and paper and fishing bottles out of the bushes; she complained that she was disappointed with the financial result, considering the influx of people. I pointed out that it was difficult to have a 'popular' fête and also make money, and that the important thing was to try to attract people who not only had some means but who were also prepared to part with their cash.

So it was that the posters for the next *festa* were of modest size and colouring, with the invitations printed on cards bearing a line drawing of the *castello*. On many of them we wrote the names of the recipients, culled mostly from the telephone book. This went down well, and from all sides we learned that the neighbourhood was looking forward to the day, especially as we expected the Florentine halberdiers, those delightful drummers in colourful mediaeval costume with plumes in the helmet of the officer in charge; they parade at Florentine *festas* and the yearly football match in the Piazza della Signoria. But, alas, on the day the sky was menacing, and as the first car-loads arrived a violent storm broke, with rather frightening thunder and flashes of lightning, so that those who had already arrived turned tail and fled down the hill, causing much havoc to the traffic. The rest of us huddled into the covered part of the courtyard, the organizer almost in tears, thinking of all the expenses which would remain uncovered.

None the less, when the worst was over and the sky cleared a little others did arrive, and those who came were generous, even though it was so damp underfoot and the halberdier captain's feathers drooped, while the drummers and the flag bearers drilled to a small and bedraggled group of spectators. It was sad that the weather had been so unkind to the first really well-organized fête.

There was a *festa* of another, more intimate, kind, when Jelly d'Aranyi held her last concert at Trebbio, together with her niece Adrienne Camilloni Fachiri. That evening at the close of the concert, with a rising full moon and a windless calm, and with the flares lit again round the tower and the rampart embrasures, the scene for the homebound guests was enchanting, with a fairy-like quality. It was an unforgettable evening.

But what of the land? Agriculture in Italy had for years been running at a loss, and farming in the hills is still a liability because it can never be converted into a kind of industry as it can where there are acres of good level ground. Little by little the farms became empty. The young peasants were dissatisfied with their life, and their families tended to establish themselves in the vicinity of the new factories springing up near Florence, while those who remained were uneasy; they missed their neighbours, and felt that they too should hurry off to better their economic position. They were loath to send their children to mind the sheep, as they could now stay at school for further education. The young farmers could not find wives to their liking, and so, inevitably, the farmsteads emptied and grass grew between the flag-stones.

In 1967 there was only one farming family left on the estate: it was that of Guglielmo Cavichi, whose farm, 'Vivaio', was within hailing distance of the *castello*, on the old pack road from Florence. It had once been a stopping-place for travellers and merchants on their way over the Apennines to Bologna. Guglielmo loved the land, for his family had for centuries farmed in the vicinity; he had fought in the 1914–1918 war and had been left with a withered right arm. But he had three stalwart sons, grand workers, and they left no inch of their earth uncultivated. Theirs was always the farm which yielded most. His wife was an excellent, strong woman, who cared for her family, and, besides making cheeses and conserves, once a year when the pig or pigs were slaughtered was busy preparing hams and sausages and other things for all. When the family needed clothes, they withdrew the sum required from the 'bank', or administrative office, at Cafaggiolo, and when necessary they could also obtain a loan. Occasionally we were invited to join them in their gregarious feasts. But eventually this family too felt the lure of the city. Poor Guglielmo was desperate at the thought of leaving; he was old and ill, and the family held on awhile, though eventual change was inevitable. Mercifully he died, as he wished, at 'Vivaio', and with him went the last and the best of the *capoccia*, with their many good qualities of diligence, prudence and—in their own field—intelligence. The speculative ingenuity of the Tuscan peasant, and his cupidity, must, I feel, have been the result of hundreds of years of subterfuge, rendered necessary for survival in bygone times, when the means of livelihood were so precarious.

Another remarkable figure was Assunta, the wife of a far less able *capoccia* who was frequently 'in the red' with the administration. She was small, wiry, voluble and tireless, and she raised eleven children. During the war her courage never left her, though her only grown son was taken into the army, and the next five of the family were all girls. They often had very little to eat, but even so Assunta ran from house to house helping the sick or giving injections, and she taught her children righteous living and strict honesty.

We still have Celeste with us, the mother of our excellent

tractor-driver-cum-electrician. Stout, economical of speech, slow of movement and suspicious alike of newcomer or of novelty, she is the exact opposite of Assunta. Until a few years ago she baked her bread every Saturday in her brick-domed oven, making the sign of the cross on the closed oven door with the end of her long-handled bread shovel. She still goes around picking up sticks and collecting chicory, a sort of edible dandelion leaf which she gathers in the fields.

Then there was dear old Ricci, who was among the last to leave. He would never see a doctor—he was quite adamant about it. When he was old and ill, one of his grandsons crept up to his bedside to tell him that they had sent for the doctor, at which news he struggled up, dressed, and hid in the oxen's stall; nothing could persuade him to leave till the 'danger' had been removed.

There came a very sad time for us. Enrico's health had been a worry ever since his taxing visits to America, and eventually, after some weeks of illness, we lost our guide, protector and friend. At least he did not live to see the disintegration at Trebbio of the *mezzadria* system, which brought so many of our hopes to an end, even though we realized that the march of time and destiny cannot, in the long run, be other than salutary for mankind. No oxen turned the sod, no shout of 'Heu-yah!' echoed across the land, and grass and weeds grew high where the wheat should have been. Gone were the orange-gold corncobs and the red of the tomatoes, while the olives grew thick and bushy for want of pruning and the long strands of the untended vines swept the ground. The woodland paths became overgrown and brambles impeded our passage, while rainstorms transformed the rural roads into grooved river-beds. The water-troughs became choked or the flow of the water was diverted, and in summer the birds ate the fruit off our trees. The bells of the homing sheep and cattle were silent, and it seemed to be the end of everything that mattered. Pompilio, our agent, had left us, his health undermined by the anxieties of the war, and half the property—all the lower part and Cafaggiolo—had been sold and the *fattoria* transferred to Trebbio, below the *castello*.

Since then our landscape has changed: instead of vineyards and rows of vines between the wheat or maize we have open fields for the grazing of sheep and country-bred horses. The corncobs are seen no more, the less important crops can no longer be grown, and some of the older olive trees, planted centuries ago, have had to make way for the tractor. But now that Lorenzo and Virginia have taken on the administration of the reduced property the tide of retreat has at last been halted, and after ten years or more the new beginning has been established.

As the urban suburbs of Prato and Firenze sprang up round the newly established factories they were occupied largely by a rural population, lured by the promise of good wages; but before very long the congestion, clamour and nervous strain of modern city life became a burden to them. As agricultural wages improved they turned their thoughts to more peaceful areas. Thus it was that little by little our deserted farms were divided and converted for modern living, and rented for holidays or weekends by these industrial families escaping the heat and turmoil of the cities. At times there are even applicants from the erstwhile peasant families who for centuries had farmed the land.

At first there was too much noise, and the proud owners of cars rushed up our steep hill with much horn-blowing, dust, litter and blaring of radios. Appreciation of the country came slowly, and we were apt to find many discarded objects in the fields, such as a bedstead, a stove, or a perambulator. But rules were imposed, and other ways of encouraging rural calm, and gradually the new inhabitants are absorbing the spirit of this oasis of beauty, and are even making small gardens—in Italy a new pastime.

Only the occasional roar of a supersonic plane, flying too low, disturbs the silence, and, alas, the soul-searing rasp of the electric motor-saw in the woodlands, and here and there the inevitable barbed wire, frustrating to those who still enjoy walking. But all is being assimilated on a newly integrated basis, though problems of complicated, obligatory administration sometimes impede and limit development.

None the less, there is still much to enjoy for those who can appreciate this upland paradise. May the growing generation be able to absorb the beauties of Nature's quiet with all the lessons she can teach them, for are not they the precursors of the New Age beyond the insecurity, the frantic strivings and the new dangers of today? The dawn does not change, and often at Trebbio the sun rises over the mountains on to a thick mist which covers the entire floor of the Mugello. The Apennine range rises up beyond as though from the far shore of this smooth sea of cloud, which infiltrates between our nearby hills, making them appear like promontories sloping down into a white and silent sea. The tower of the little church opposite us (now closed, its bells silent) at such times stands bravely as though on a small island defying the encroachment of the waters or like a ship riding the waves. I have been told that our panorama is akin to vast views in parts of China, with only the pagodas missing from the summits of the little hills; instead there is a ruined tower or a clump of trees. I am reminded of a translation of a Chinese poem, a favourite:

> Swiftly the years, beyond recall.
> Solemn the stillness of this fair morning.
> I will clothe myself in spring-clothing
> And visit the slopes of the Eastern Hill.
> By the mountain-stream a mist hovers,
> Hovers a moment, then scatters.
> There comes a wind blowing from the south
> That brushes the fields of new corn.

There are glorious evenings when the *castello* stands out above the encircling dark cypress trees to catch the light of the setting sun; the humped tiles of the roof are still of russet, yellow, ochre and green, the walls a soft pink in the sunset, and in the winter the shadows of the trees against the stucco of the walls are mauve in hue. The August moon in her fullness shines bright and seems so much larger than usual, for her passage is low in the sky . . . and the hoopoes have returned. There can still be peace.

SONNET TO TREBBIO

From Cosimo's tall tower we see again
   Wide forests, battlements, and sweeping hills,
   Landscape of History, that for ever fills
The mind with past magnificence and pain.
Where Dante made dark music, Angelo
   Prisoned his souls in stone, painters portrayed
   The love, hate, grandeur of which life is made,
Catching a gleam of heaven here below.

The great—also the faithful few, who save
   The past from sinking slowly to the grave,
Are they upon whom human joy depends.
   Your house, your home, yourselves unknowingly have
A part in History, when love extends
Such dear, warm-hearted welcome to your friends.

TOM GAUNT